FOR WRITING GRADES K–3

SEP 9362

30 Graphic Organizers

WITH LESSONS & TRANSPARENCIES

Prewriting

Drafting

Publishing

Editing

Revising

Shell Educational Publishing

Author

Christi E. Parker, M.A.Ed.

Shell Educational Publishing

Editor
Christina Hill

Project Manager
Gillian Eve Makepeace

Editorial Director
Emily R. Smith, M.A.Ed.

Editor-in-Chief
Sharon Coan, M.S.Ed.

Creative Director
Lee Aucoin

Production Manager
Peter Pulido

Imaging
Misty Shaw

Illustration Manager
Timothy J. Bradley

Cover Artist
Lesley Palmer

Standards
Compendium, ©2004 McREL

Publisher
Corinne Burton, M.A.Ed

Shell Educational Publishing

5301 Oceanus Drive

Huntington Beach, CA 92649-1030

http://www.seppub.com

ISBN-0-7439-9362-4

Table of Contents

Introduction

Graphic Organizers 4–6

Bloom's Taxonomy 7–8

Combining Graphic Organizers
and Bloom's Taxonomy 8–9

Correlation to Standards 9–11

How to Use This Book 12–13

Lesson Flow Chart 14

Prewriting

Shopping for Ideas
Graphic Organizer 15–18

The Rhyme Climb
Graphic Organizer 19–22

Bright Ideas Graphic Organizer 23–26

Stories to Tell Graphic Organizer 27–30

Doorway to Drawings
Graphic Organizer 31–34

Snapshots of Me Graphic Organizer . . . 35–38

Drafting

A Shower of Words
Graphic Organizer 39–42

Words from the Wise
Graphic Organizer 43–46

Along the Way Graphic Organizer 47–50

Take Action Graphic Organizer 51–54

Poetry in Motion Graphic Organizer . . . 55–58

Building a Letter Graphic Organizer . . . 59–62

Editing

The Name Game Graphic Organizer . . . 63–66

Look It Up Graphic Organizer 67–70

Mr. Fix It Graphic Organizer 71–74

At the End of the Rope
Graphic Organizer 75–78

Editing (cont.)

Puzzle Pieces Graphic Organizer 79–82

At the Car Wash Graphic Organizer . . . 83–86

Revising

Like a Sore Thumb
Graphic Organizer 87–90

The Strongest Word
Graphic Organizer 91–94

Vegetable Variety Graphic Organizer . . 95–98

One More Time Graphic Organizer . . . 99–102

Ask Me Anything
Graphic Organizer 103–106

Lending a Hand
Graphic Organizer 107–110

Publishing

Share the Love Graphic Organizer . . 111–114

In the Mail Graphic Organizer 115–118

Memory Makers
Graphic Organizer 119–122

Tell Me a Story
Graphic Organizer 123–126

Having a Ball Graphic Organizer . . . 127–130

Picture This Graphic Organizer 131–134

Appendix

Works Cited 135

Graphic Organizer Flip Book 136–144

Graphic Organizer Overheads

This section contains a copy of each blank graphic organizer. These 30 overhead transparencies are in the same order as the lessons in the book.

Introduction

Graphic Organizers

When working with students, what is the best way to have them classify different kinds of animals? How about getting them to explain the connections between certain characters in a story? How can teachers help students make broad connections between math concepts? Can students ever successfully differentiate between the different instruments in a band?

One way to improve students' learning and performance across the grade levels in a wide range of content areas with diverse students is by utilizing graphic organizers in the classroom. Graphic organizers are visual representations that help gather and sort information. They help students see patterns and relationships between the given information. With only a few words, concepts are clarified, information and ideas are organized, and complex relationships are shown between the elements. Also, as an added bonus, graphic organizers help teachers figure out how students think.

More often than not, these organizers are referred to as maps because they help "map out" ideas in a visual way. In recent years, graphic organizers have taken on various names including semantic maps, webs, concept maps, story maps, and semantic organizers. Some examples of commonly used graphic organizers include spider maps, Venn diagrams, T-charts, and KWL charts. Perhaps the most widely used graphic organizer is the calendar. Calendars help sort, sift, record, and share information. In this series, the authors have gone beyond the common organizers seen in the past and created lessons that use more unique graphic organizers.

How do graphic organizers work? Graphic organizers have a way of connecting several pieces of isolated information. They take new information and file it into an existing framework. Old information is retrieved in the process, and the new information is attached. This is positive news for the classroom teacher who has her students using graphic organizers. By using these organizers, she is helping her students make connections and assimilate new information into what they already know. In effect, she is providing her students with a mental filing cabinet where their knowledge can be easily stored and retrieved.

Understanding how the brain works helps to understand why graphic organizers are valuable tools for learning. Educational brain research says that the brain seeks patterns so that information can be made meaningful. In her book, Karen Olsen (1995) states, "From brain research we have come to understand that the brain is a pattern-seeking device in search of meaning and that learning is the acquisition of mental programs for using what we understand."

Graphic Organizers *(cont.)*

Other researchers believe that graphic organizers are one of the most powerful ways to build semantic memories (Sprenger 1999). Eric Jensen (1998) states that semantic memory is "activated by association, similarities, or contrasts." Graphic organizers assist students with such necessary connections.

How does the brain do this? The brain stores information similar to how a graphic organizer shows information. It screens large amounts of information and looks for patterns that are linked together. The brain is able to extract meaning much easier from a visual format like a graphic organizer than from written words on a page. Graphic organizers not only help students manage information, but they offer information in a way that students can understand at a glance. When connections are made on paper, the information engages other parts of the brain. When these connections happen, the brain transfers the information from short-term memory to long-term memory.

So what does this mean for classroom teachers? It means that teachers who use graphic organizers help their students manage all the information they are presented with each day. These organizers record important pieces of information that students can connect with previous information and build upon for future information.

There is more good news for teachers who are looking to develop their students' reading skills. Research suggests that graphic organizers improve the students' overall reading abilities. When graphic organizers are used, reading comprehension improves (Sinatra et al. 1984; Brookbank et al. 1999). In fact, the National Reading Panel (2000) included graphic organizers in its list of effective instructional tools to improve reading comprehension.

Researchers also find that students at all levels are mastering key vocabulary skills when graphic organizers are used as teaching aids (Brookbank et al. 1999; Moore and Readence 1984). How does this happen? As previously stated, graphic organizers take new knowledge and integrate it with prior knowledge so that students can make connections and comprehend the material. So, graphic organizers help students focus on vocabulary development rather than the other reading skills.

For those teachers who look for ways to improve their students' writing abilities, graphic organizers do this as well. Studies performed with second and third graders showed that their writing skills improved when graphic organizers were incorporated as part of the writing process (Gallick-Jackson 1997). How do graphic organizers help to improve writing? When students fill out graphic organizers, they learn to summarize information and take notes more efficiently. When used in place of an outlining tool, graphic organizers make students think about how to write the new information in a different way.

Graphic Organizers *(cont.)*

The information written on these organizers becomes personal as students write it in their own words. Organizers also provide a unique way for students to take notes during a lecture or while reading a passage. This is a skill that is useful throughout life. When teachers help students to see that they only need to write the information that they want to remember, students also begin to assess and evaluate what they already know.

Teachers who want to increase their students' thinking and learning skills should also use graphic organizers. One way to improve students' critical and creative thinking skills is by using graphic organizers while working on classroom projects (Brookbank et al. 1999; DeWispelaere and Kossack 1996). Especially when used with brainstorming, graphic organizers can help students generate creative ideas. Graphic organizers also help students clarify their thinking. Students use organizers to demonstrate their understanding of a topic.

Various types of graphic organizers serve as effective evaluation documents at the end of a unit. Most teachers struggle just getting their students to retain what they have learned. Graphic organizers provide a way for students to discover and retain new information (Bos and Anders 1992; Ritchie and Volkl 2000; Griffin et al. 1995).

Graphic organizers also complement many different learning styles. Teachers are faced every day with a diverse population of students who learn in different ways. Many of these students are visual learners. Visual learners remember information better through images like those created through graphic organizers. Students develop the habit of thinking in terms of symbols or key words. Not only are graphic organizers a great tool for visual thinkers, they are a great tool for helping all students become stronger visual thinkers.

Finally, teachers are able to meet the needs of their diverse learners with graphic organizers. Studies indicate that graphic organizers benefit students with learning disabilities (Boyle and Weishaar 1997; Doyle 1999; Gallego et al. 1989; Gardill and Jitendra 1999; Griffin et al. 1991; Sinatra et al. 1984). In these studies, learning-disabled students understood content-area material, organized information, and retained and recalled information better when using graphic organizers. As a result, graphic organizers have become a great tool for classroom teachers who need to differentiate the materials.

Overall, researchers and teachers alike have found that the use of graphic organizers is beneficial to student learning. Not only do graphic organizers make learning more interesting and varied, but students' ability to retain and recall learning is increased. Teachers will find, when using graphic organizers like the ones in this book, that their students are more willing and able to meet their classroom learning standards.

Introduction *(cont.)*

Bloom's Taxonomy

In 1956, educator Benjamin Bloom worked with a group of educational psychologists to classify levels of cognitive thinking. The levels they named are knowledge, comprehension, application, analysis, synthesis, and evaluation. Bloom's Taxonomy has been used in classrooms over the last 40 years as a hierarchy of questions that progress from easy to more complex. The progression allows teachers to identify the level at which students are thinking. It also provides a framework for introducing a variety of questions and activities to students.

Many teachers see this taxonomy as a ladder. For example, some teachers think they must begin at the bottom with knowledge questions and work their way progressively up to the evaluative questions. But that is not necessary to achieve good questions for students. There are appropriate times for each level of questioning.

The taxonomy is a useful model for categorizing questions and classroom activities. The following paragraphs describe each of the levels of the taxonomy in more detail.

Knowledge—The knowledge cognitive skill requires that students recall or locate information, remember something previously learned, and memorize information. Some specific examples of knowledge in the classroom would include writing the definitions of words or labeling the planets in the solar system.

Comprehension—The comprehension cognitive skill requires that students understand and explain facts, demonstrate basic understanding of concepts and curriculum, translate facts into other words, grasp meanings, interpret information, or explain what happened in their own words (or pictures). Some specific examples of comprehension in the classroom would include describing the reasons clouds rain or summarizing a chapter of a story.

Application—The application cognitive skill requires that students use prior learning to solve a problem or to answer a question, transfer knowledge learned in one situation to another, use different material in new and concrete situations, and apply the lessons of the past to a situation today. A specific example of application would include taking specific data and putting it into a bar graph.

Analysis—The analysis cognitive skill requires that students see in-depth relationships, understand how parts relate to a whole, and break down material into its component parts. Some specific examples of analysis would include comparing and contrasting the current president's campaign promises to those of President Abraham Lincoln or finding out the ways that a large influx of immigrants might change a community.

Bloom's Taxonomy *(cont.)*

Synthesis—The synthesis cognitive skill requires that students create new ideas by pulling parts of the information together, reform individual parts to make a new whole, and take a jumble of facts and combine them until they make sense. Some specific examples of synthesis in the classroom include creating a new song about the continents or writing a new ending to a book.

Evaluation—The evaluation cognitive skill requires that students make judgments based on evidence, judge the value of something, support judgments, and examine something and decide whether it measures up to a certain standard. Some specific examples of evaluation in the classroom include justifying the decision made to require homework every night or deciding whether to agree or disagree with the statement "lying is always bad."

Combining Graphic Organizers and Bloom's Taxonomy

Using graphic organizers with effective questioning techniques creates an added bonus to any curriculum. This combination takes lessons in the classroom to the next level of excellence. In effect, lessons that combine graphic organizers and Bloom's Taxonomy create an ideal learning experience for students. The outcome is differentiated material that meets the needs of all students and engages students.

Utilizing graphic organizers while getting students to think on different levels, creates a more complex and engaging lesson for students. When a teacher needs her students to apply the information they just learned, she can use a graphic organizer that correlates with the application level of Bloom's Taxonomy. Or, the teacher can touch on multiple levels of the taxonomy. A graphic organizer might require students to fill in a chart to show their knowlege about and comprehension of the material. Then, they have to evaluate what they have written in a sentence or two. Think about the benefits of using graphic organizers to increase vocabulary skills while knowing how to ask different levels of questions to improve thinking skills at the same time. Imagine improving writing with graphic organizers and also getting students to analyze that writing. Students can learn how to take better notes and place them in an organizer that immediately helps them evaluate what they have written.

Critical thinking skills are a by-product of both graphic organizers and Bloom's Taxonomy. These two strategies mesh perfectly together and help students to think more effectively. Finally, using both of these strategies meets the needs of diverse students, including those with learning disabilities. All students can find ways to communicate their knowledge at various levels of learning and thinking.

Combining Graphic Organizers and Bloom's Taxonomy *(cont.)*

The lessons in this book show how to easily align graphic organizers with Bloom's Taxonomy. These lessons are organized into five different content areas. For each of these areas, a lesson that correlates with each level of Bloom's Taxonomy is provided. Each lesson includes general directions, a blank copy of the graphic organizer, an overhead transparency (located in order in the back of the book), and a sample lesson along with a completed sample graphic organizer.

Correlation to Standards

Shell Educational Publishing (SEP) is committed to producing educational materials that are research and standards based. In this effort, the company uses the Mid-continent Research for Education and Learning (McREL) Standards Compendium. Each year, McREL analyzes state standards and revises the compendium. By following this procedure, McREL produces a general compilation of national standards. Each lesson in this book is based on a McREL standard. Then, the product is correlated to the academic standards of all 50 states, the District of Columbia, and the Department of Defense Dependent Schools. You can print a correlation report customized for your state directly from the SEP website at **http://www.seppub.com**.

Purpose and Intent of Standards

The No Child Left Behind (NCLB) legislation mandates that all states adopt academic standards that identify the skills students will learn in kindergarten through grade twelve. While many states had already adopted academic standards prior to NCLB, the legislation requirements ensure that state standards are detailed and comprehensive.

Standards are designed to focus instruction and guide adoption of curricula. Standards are statements that describe the criteria necessary for students to meet specific academic goals. They define the knowledge, skills, and content students should acquire at each grade level. Standards are also used to develop standardized tests to evaluate students' academic progress. In many states today, teachers are required to demonstrate how their lessons meet state standards. State standards are used in the planning and development of all SEP products. So, educators can be assured the products meet their academic requirements.

How to Find Standards Correlations

Complete standards correlation reports for each state can be printed from the SEP website. To print a correlation report for this product visit the website at **http://www.seppub.com** and follow the on-screen directions. For assistance in printing correlation reports, please contact Customer Service at 1-877-777-3450.

Introduction *(cont.)*

Correlation to Standards *(cont.)*

Unless otherwise noted, the McREL standards listed in this book are taken from the Level I (Grades K–2) Language Arts standards. The number listed for each standard (e.g., 6.3) refers to the standard number and the benchmark within the standard.

Graphic Organizer	Lesson Title	McREL Content Standard
Shopping for Ideas	Shopping for Science	Prewriting: Uses prewriting strategies to plan written work (e.g., writes key thoughts). (McREL Language Arts, Standard 1.1)
The Rhyme Climb	How Do the Rhymes End?	Prewriting: Recites and responds to familiar stories, poems, and rhymes with patterns. (McREL Language Arts, Standard 8.7)
Bright Ideas	Bright Toy Ideas	Prewriting: Uses prewriting strategies to plan written work (e.g., discusses ideas with peers). (McREL Language Arts, Standard 1.1)
Stories to Tell	Family Moments to Tell	Prewriting: Uses writing and other methods (making lists) to describe familiar person, places, objects, or experiences. (McREL Language Arts, Standard 1.6)
Doorway to Drawings	Doorway to Family Drawings	Prewriting: Uses prewriting strategies to plan written work (e.g., draws pictures to generate ideas). (McREL Language Arts, Standard 1.1)
Snapshots of Me	Sending Snapshots to Another Class	Prewriting: Uses prewriting strategies to plan written work (e.g., records observations.). (McREL Language Arts, Standard 1.1)
A Shower of Words	A Shower of Toys	Drafting: Uses adjectives in written compositions (e.g., uses descriptive words). (McREL Language Arts, Standard 3.5)
Words from the Wise	Wise Science Words	Drafting: Writes in a variety of forms or genres (e.g., information pieces). (McREL Language Arts, Standard 1.7)
Along the Way	Along the Way to Family Memories	Drafting: Uses strategies to organize written work (e.g., uses a sequence of events). (McREL Language Arts, Standard 1.5)
Take Action	Take Family Action	Drafting: Knows setting, main characters, main events, sequence, and problems in stories. (McREL Language Arts, Standard 6.3)
Poetry in Motion	Animals in Motion	Drafting: Writes in a variety of forms or genres (e.g., poems). (McREL Language Arts, Standard 1.7)
Building a Letter	Building a Pen Pal Letter	Drafting: Writes in a variety of forms or genres (friendly letters). (McREL Language Arts, Standard 1.7)
The Name Game	The First and Last Name Game	Editing: Uses conventions of capitalization in written compositions (e.g., first and last names). (McREL Language Arts, Standard 3.8)
Look It Up	Looking It Up with Peers	Editing: Uses conventions of spelling in written compositions (e.g., uses a dictionary and other resources to spell words). (McREL Language Arts, Standard 3.7)
Mr. Fix It	Fixing Family Memories	Editing: Evaluates own and others' writing (e.g., asks questions and makes comments about writing, helps classmates apply grammatical and mechanical conventions). (McREL Language Arts, Standard 1.4)

Introduction *(cont.)*

Correlation to Standards *(cont.)*

Graphic Organizer	Lesson Title	McREL Content Standard
At the End of the Rope	At the End of the Science Rope	Editing: Uses conventions of punctuation in written compositions (e.g., uses periods after declarative sentences, uses question marks after interrogative sentences). (McREL Language Arts, Standard 3.9)
Puzzle Pieces	Family Puzzle Pieces	Editing: Uses complete sentences in written compositions. (McREL Language Arts, Standard 3.2)
At the Car Wash	At the Animal Car Wash	Editing: Uses strategies to draft and revise written work (rearranges words to improve or clarify meaning). (McREL Language Arts, Standard 1.2)
Like a Sore Thumb	The Sore Thumb of Family Memories	Revising: Uses strategies to draft and revise written work (e.g., deletes extraneous information). (McREL Language Arts, Standard 1.2)
The Strongest Word	The Family's Strongest Word	Revising: Uses verbs in written compositions (e.g., verbs for a variety of situations, action words). (McREL Language Arts, Standard 3.4)
Vegetable Variety	A Variety of Pen Pal Letters	Revising: Uses strategies to draft and revise written work (e.g., varies sentence type). (McREL Language Arts, Standard 1.2)
One More Time	Reading About Science One More Time	Revising: Uses strategies to draft and revise written work (e.g., rereads). (McREL Language Arts, Standard 1.2)
Ask Me Anything	Ask the Animals Anything	Revising: Evaluates own and others' writing (e.g., asks questions about writing). (McREL Language Arts, Standard 1.4)
Lending a Hand	Lending a Hand for Toys	Revising: Uses strategies to draft and revise written work (e.g., incorporates suggestions from peers and teachers). (McREL Language Arts, Standard 1.2)
Share the Love	Share the Love of Toys	Publishing: Uses strategies to edit and publish written work (e.g., shares finished product). (McREL Language Arts, Standard 1.3)
In the Mail	It's in the Mail to My Pen Pal	Publishing: Writes personal letters (e.g., addresses envelopes). (McREL Language Arts, Standard 1.12, Level II)
Memory Makers	Family Memory Makers	Publishing: Knows the main ideas or themes of a story. (McREL Language Arts, Standard 6.4)
Tell Me a Story	Tell Me a Family Story	Publishing: Knows setting, main characters, main events, sequence, and problems in stories. (McREL Language Arts, Standard 6.3)
Having a Ball	Having an Animal Ball	Publishing: Uses strategies to edit and publish written work (e.g., incorporates illustrations or photos). (McREL Language Arts, Standard 1.3)
Picture This	Picture My Science Topic	Publishing: Uses mental images based on pictures and print to aid in comprehension of text. (McREL Language Arts, Standard 5.1)

Introduction *(cont.)*

How to Use This Book

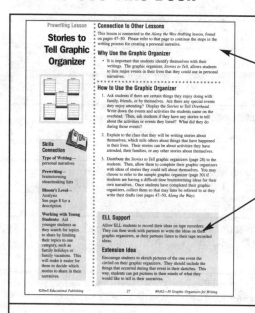

General Information on the Graphic Organizer

Why and How to Use the Graphic Organizer

- This part of the lesson plan gives general information about ways in which the graphic organizer will benefit your classroom. It also lists step-by-step directions for using the blank organizer.

ELL Support and Extension Idea

- For each lesson, suggestions are given to better utilize the graphic organizer with second-language learners. Ideas of ways to extend the lesson are also given for more advanced students or those who finish the activities early.

Blank Graphic Organizer

- You are provided with a blank copy of each graphic organizer so that you can repeatedly use the lesson with your students. Both the general lessons and the specific lessons describe how you may want to use the blank copy.

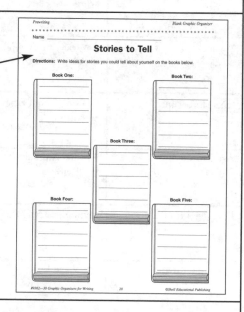

Graphic Organizer Overheads

- You are provided with a blank copy of each graphic organizer. You can use the overheads to model exactly how to use each of the graphic organizers.

- The graphic organizer overheads are located in the back of the book. They are in the same order as the lessons. The titles on the overheads match the titles on the blank graphic organizers to make them easy to locate. In the header of the overheads is a page reference back to the lesson in the book.

- Once you begin using these lessons, you may find that you want to start a three-ring notebook for keeping the overhead transparencies in order.

How to Use This Book *(cont.)*

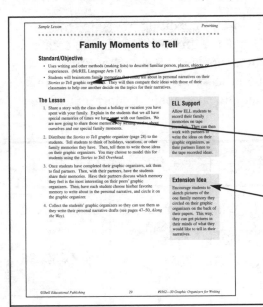

Example Lesson Using the Graphic Organizer

Standard/Objective

- Each example lesson covers one skill in the writing process. A general language arts standard is listed along with a specific learning objective.

The Lesson

- The lesson section describes specifically how to use the graphic organizer for teaching that writing skill.

ELL Support and Extension Idea

- For each lesson, suggestions are given to better utilize the graphic organizer with second-language learners. Ideas of ways to extend the lesson are also given for more advanced students or those who finish the activities early.

Example Graphic Organizer

- You are provided with a completed example of each graphic organizer. The example is based on the chosen piece of children's literature so that you have a model for the students as they work.

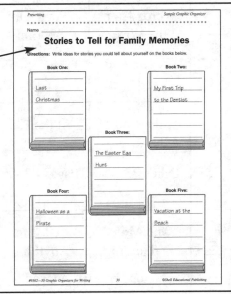

Graphic Organizer Flip Book

Definition

- Each level of Bloom's Taxonomy is defined for easy reference.

Verbs

- A list of verbs is included to help teachers plan appropriate activities for each level of Bloom's Taxonomy.

Thumbnails

- The flip book is intended to help you easily find and plan both high- and low-level activities. You can decide what kinds of lessons you would like to use and then reference the flip book to choose lessons from this book or plan your own.

Introduction *(cont.)*

Lesson Flow Chart

This book covers the five steps of the writing process: prewriting, drafting, editing, revising, and publishing. Although there are 30 individual graphic organizers, they are grouped together to create six unique writing pieces. The chart below shows how the lessons are connected. For each writing assignment, there are five lessons (one for each step in the writing process). Teachers can follow this chart to go through the entire writing process. Or, they can use individual graphic organizers to focus on single steps in the process.

	1	2	3	4	5	6
Prewriting	Shopping for Ideas Pages 15–18	The Rhyme Climb Pages 19–22	Bright Ideas Pages 23–26	Stories to Tell Pages 27–30	Doorway to Drawings Pages 31–34	Snapshots of Me Pages 35–38
Drafting	Words from the Wise Pages 43–46	Poetry in Motion Pages 55–58	A Shower of Words Pages 39–42	Along the Way Pages 47–50	Take Action Pages 51–54	Building a Letter Pages 59–62
Editing	At the End of the Rope Pages 75–78	At the Car Wash Pages 83–86	Look It Up Pages 67–70	Mr. Fix It Pages 71–74	Puzzle Pieces Pages 79–82	The Name Game Pages 63–66
Revising	One More Time Pages 99–102	Ask Me Anything Pages 103–106	Lending a Hand Pages 107–110	Like a Sore Thumb Pages 87–90	The Strongest Word Pages 91–94	Vegetable Variety Pages 95–98
Publishing	Picture This Pages 131–134	Having a Ball Pages 127–130	Share the Love Pages 111–114	Memory Makers Pages 119–122	Tell Me a Story Pages 123–126	In the Mail Pages 115–118

Informational — Poetry — Descriptive — Narrative — Picture Book — Friendly Letter

Shopping for Ideas Graphic Organizer

Skills Connection

Type of Writing— informational

Prewriting—writing key thoughts

Bloom's Level— Knowledge (See page 7 for a description.)

Working with Young Students: Choose topics for younger students to write about in their *informational* pieces, rather than allowing them to choose. You might want to choose topics from units they are currently studying.

Why Use the Graphic Organizer

- The *Shopping for Ideas* graphic organizer allows students to organize their thoughts and ideas, so that they can later choose topics for *informational* writing pieces.

How to Use the Graphic Organizer

1. Show students a photograph related to a topic they have recently studied. Then, ask them to tell you everything they know about the topic. Write their thoughts on the board.

2. Display the *Shopping for Ideas Overhead* so that the class can see it. Then, ask them to list other topics that they know a lot about. List some of their ideas on the overhead.

3. Tell the class that they will be writing *informational* pieces that will tell others about topics in which they are experts. Distribute the *Shopping for Ideas* graphic organizers (page 16) to the students. Ask them to list the items they would like to tell others about on their graphic organizers.

4. Then, ask the students to circle the one item on their organizers about which they would like to inform others.

ELL Support

Allow ELL students to walk around the room, searching for items about which they could inform, or tell others. Then, have them write those items' names or draw pictures of those items on their graphic organizers.

Extension Idea

Challenge students to list only topics they have recently studied in the class, such as in social studies, thematic units, or math. This way, they are informing others of things they have learned at school.

Name _____

Shopping for Ideas

Directions: Make a list of topics that you know well. Circle the topic you would like to write more about.

• •

Shopping for Science

Standard/Objective

• **Prewriting:** Uses prewriting strategies to plan written work (e.g., writes key thoughts). (McREL Language Arts, Standard 1.1)

• Students will create lists of science topics about which they are familiar and can later use to inform others, using their *Shopping for Ideas* graphic organizers.

The Lesson

1. Ask the class what their favorite topics in science are. Write the topics they list on the *Shopping for Ideas Overhead*.

2. Tell the class that they are science experts. As science experts, they will need to inform, or tell others, about what they know concerning various science topics.

3. Distribute the *Shopping for Ideas* graphic organizers (page 16) to the students. Then, ask them to list science topics for which they are experts on their graphic organizers. Once they list the topics, ask them to circle one topic on their organizers about which they would like to inform others. You may wish to show students the sample graphic organizer (page 18) if they are struggling with science topics.

4. Then, collect their graphic organizers so they may refer to them as they write their drafts in the *Words from the Wise* lesson (pages 45–46).

ELL Support

Allow ELL students to use science books to help them find ideas of science topics. Then, have them write those topics' names, or draw small pictures of those items, on their graphic organizers.

Extension Idea

Challenge students to list only topics they have recently studied in science class. This way, they are informing others of things they have learned in school.

Connections to Other Lessons

Please refer to the following lessons to continue the steps in the process for creating *informational* writing pieces.

• *Words from the Wise*—pages 45–46
• *At the End of the Rope*—pages 77–78
• *One More Time*—pages 101–102
• *Picture This*—pages 133–134

Name _____

Shopping for Ideas for Science

Directions: Make a list of topics that you know well. Circle the topic you would like to write more about.

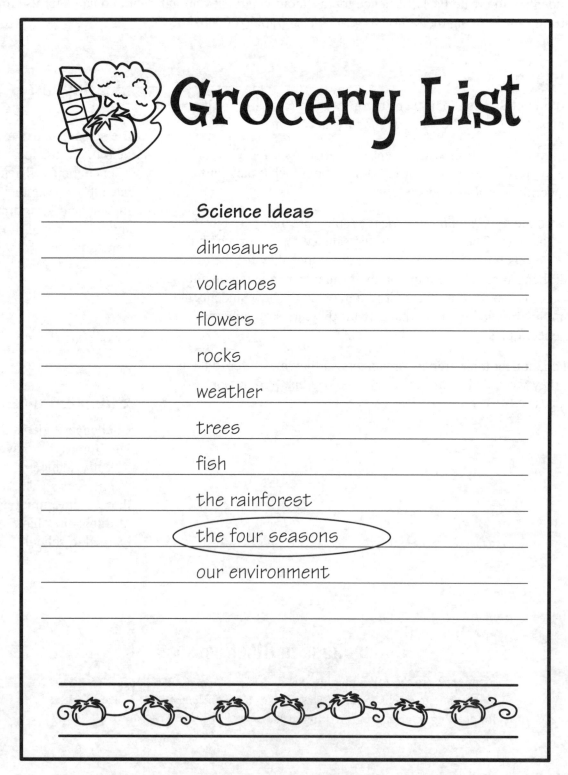

Grocery List

Science Ideas

dinosaurs

volcanoes

flowers

rocks

weather

trees

fish

the rainforest

(the four seasons)

our environment

The Rhyme Climb Graphic Organizer

Why Use the Graphic Organizer

- *The Rhyme Climb* graphic organizer allows students to visually see words that rhyme. This way, they can easily identify the word endings to those rhyming words.

How to Use the Graphic Organizer

1. Read a rhyming poem to the class. Then, explain to the class what rhyming words are.

2. Place *The Rhyme Climb Overhead* so that students can see it. Choose a word from the poem. Write the end sound of the word on the top rung of the graphic organizer. Ask the class what words rhyme with that word, or have the same ending sound. Write the rhyming words on the other rungs of the ladder.

3. Give each student a copy of *The Rhyme Climb* graphic organizer (page 20). Assign the class a word ending. Have the students list rhyming words for the word ending you assigned on their graphic organizers. You may choose for them to share their rhyming words in small groups or with the rest of the class to ensure that they indeed listed words that rhyme.

4. Explain to the class that they can use their rhyming words to create poems.

Skills Connection

Type of Writing— poetry

Prewriting—rhyming words

Bloom's Level— Comprehension (See page 7 for a description.)

Working with Young Students: Rather than asking younger students to list rhyming words on their own, list the words as a class as the students copy them onto their graphic organizers.

ELL Support

Provide ELL students with rhyming dictionaries, which they can refer to as they complete their graphic organizers.

Extension Idea

Allow students to also create original words on their graphic organizers that have the same word ending as the one assigned to the class. Then, allow them to use those words in their poems, along with real words. Their poems could be somewhat silly, using these nonsense words, similar to the poetry of Shel Silverstein.

Name _____

The Rhyme Climb

Directions: Write the word ending on the line above the ladder. Then, write words that rhyme, or have that same word ending, on the remaining rungs.

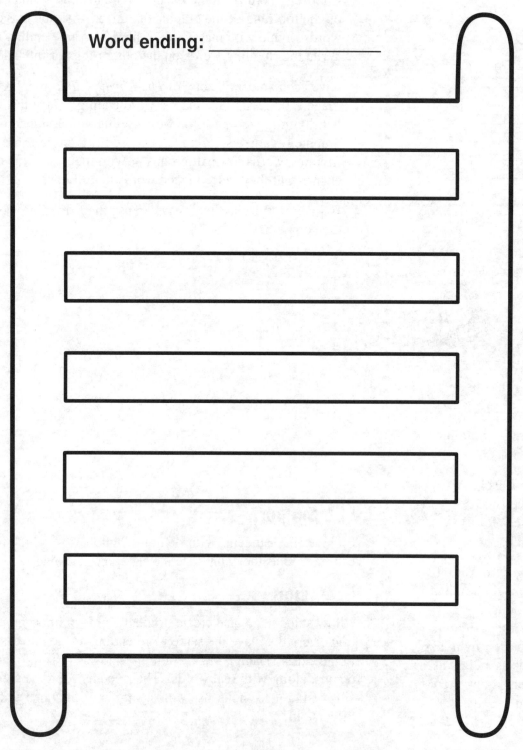

Word ending: _____

How Do the Rhymes End?

Standard/Objective

- **Prewriting:** Recites and responds to familiar stories, poems, and rhymes with patterns. (McREL Language Arts, Standard 8.7)
- Students will create lists of rhyming words that end with the –oat, –at, or –og patterns using their *The Rhyme Climb* graphic organizers.

The Lesson

1. Read students the poem, "Jumping Rope" by Shel Silverstein, taken from the book, *Where the Sidewalk Ends*.

2. Then, display *The Rhyme Climb Overhead*. Ask students to identify the end sound of the rhyming words found in the poem. Write the end sound on the top rung of the ladder. Then, complete the ladder with both the words mentioned in the poem and other –ope words.

3. Distribute *The Rhyme Climb* graphic organizers (page 20) to the students. Divide the class into three different groups. Assign one group the ending –oat, the second –at, and the third, -og. Then, ask the class to name one word that rhymes with each of the endings to get them started. You may also choose to show them the sample graphic organizer (page 22) as an example.

4. Ask the students to complete their graphic organizers with words that rhyme with their word endings. Then, ask them to share their lists in their groups or with the class.

5. Collect students' graphic organizers. Explain to them that they will use their rhyming words to create poems in the next lesson, *Poetry in Motion* (pages 57–58).

ELL Support

Provide ELL students with rhyming dictionaries, which they can refer to as they complete their graphic organizers for the word endings assigned to them.

Extension Idea

Allow students to also create original words on their graphic organizers that rhyme with the word endings assigned to them. Then, allow them to use those words in their poems, as well as real words that contain their assigned words endings. Their poems could be somewhat silly, using these nonsense words, similar to the poetry of Shel Silverstein.

Connections to Other Lessons

Please refer to the following lessons to continue the steps in the process for creating *poetry*.

- *Poetry in Motion*—pages 57–58
- *At the Car Wash*—pages 85–86
- *Ask Me Anything*—pages 105–106
- *Having a Ball*—pages 129–130

Name _____

The Rhyme Climb for Words Ending in -EE

Directions: Write the word ending on the line above the ladder. Then, write words that rhyme, or have that same word ending, on the remaining rungs.

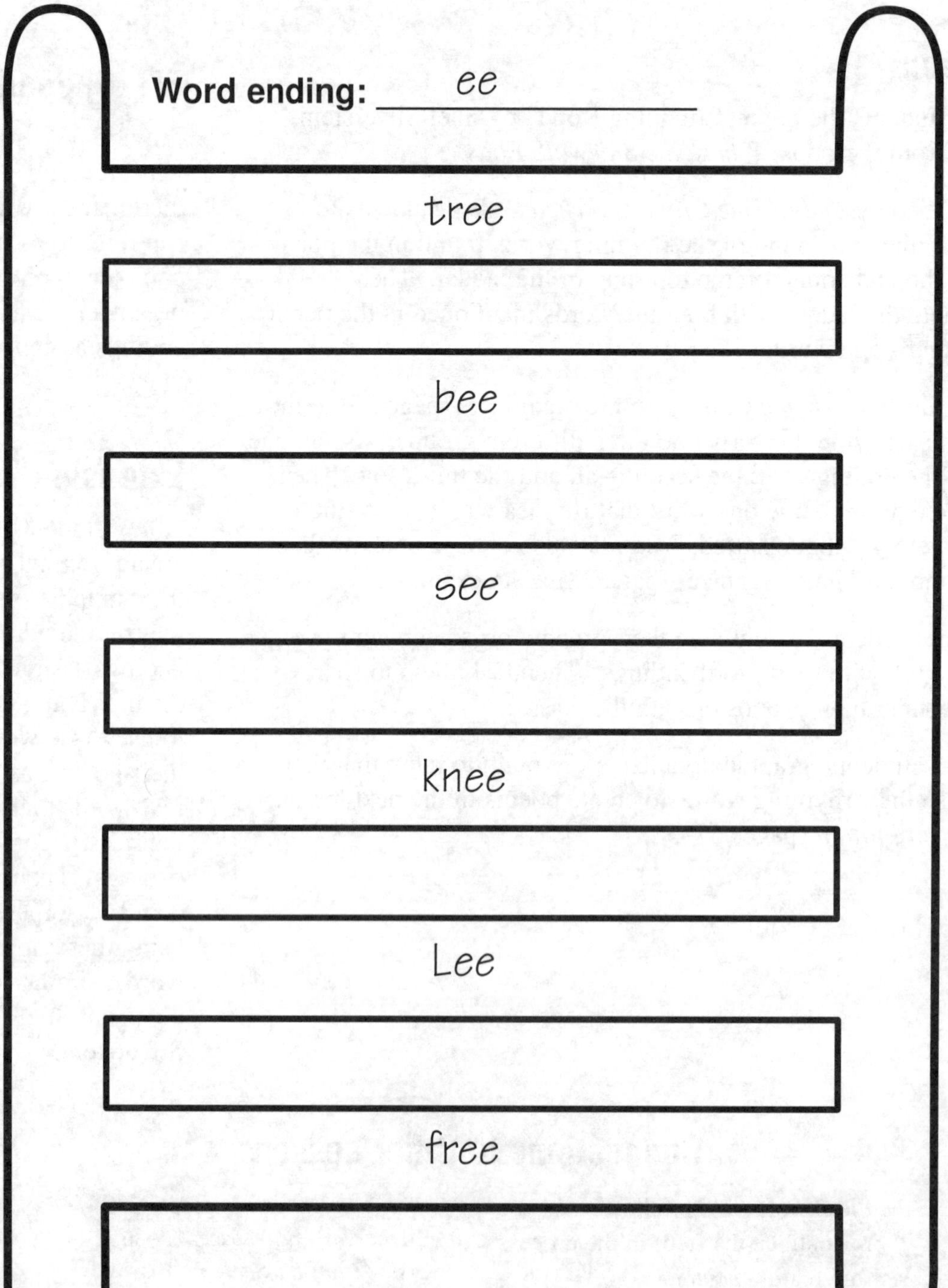

Word ending: _____ee_____

tree

bee

see

knee

Lee

free

Bright Ideas Graphic Organizer

Skills Connection

Type of Writing— descriptive

Prewriting— discussing ideas with peers

Bloom's Level— Application (See page 8 for a description.)

Working with Young Students: Ask younger students to draw pictures of items they might wish to describe, rather than writing lists. They may also use their pictures later as they write their drafts.

Why Use the Graphic Organizer

- It is often difficult for students to generate ideas for their writings. The *Bright Ideas* graphic organizer allows students to brainstorm lists of items that they would like to describe by discussing their ideas with their peers.

How to Use the Graphic Organizer

1. Bring in a stuffed animal for the class to describe. Then, ask them how they would describe the animal. *What color is it? How big is it? What makes it special or unique?*

2. Place the *Bright Ideas Overhead* so that students can see it. Also, distribute the *Bright Ideas* graphic organizers (page 24). Ask the class if there are other items that would be fun to describe. As a class, brainstorm a few more items. Record them on the overhead as students write them on their graphic organizers.

3. Allow students to form small groups to brainstorm more items to describe. Have them write their items on their graphic organizers.

4. After students have completed their graphic organizers, ask them to share some of their ideas with the class. Then, have each student circle the one item he/she wishes to describe on his or her graphic organizer.

ELL Support

Allow ELL students to look around the room for items they might wish to describe. This will help them form more ideas for their graphic organizers.

Extension Idea

Challenge students to create lists of items they might describe under certain categories, such as types of candy or things found in nature.

Name _____

Bright Ideas

Directions: Create a list of items you would like to describe on the light bulb below. Circle the item you would like to write more about.

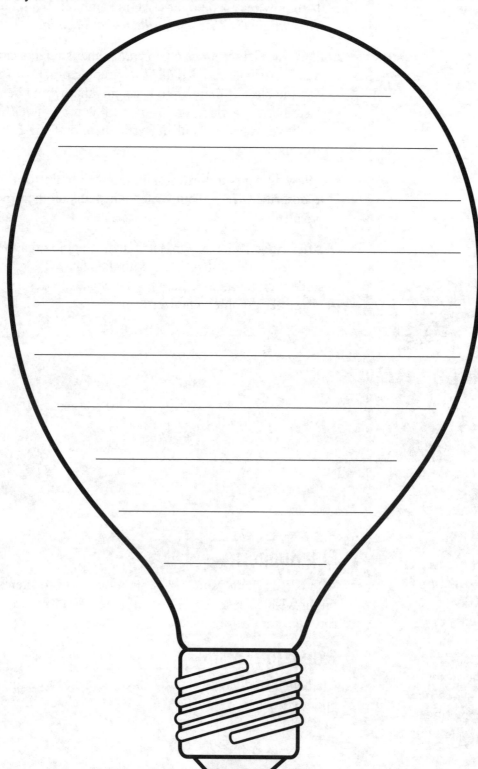

Bright Toy Ideas

Standard/Objective

- **Prewriting:** Uses prewriting strategies to plan written work (e.g., discusses ideas with peers). (McREL Language Arts, Standard 1.1)
- Students will work with their classmates to create lists of toys that would be fun to describe. They will record their ideas on their *Bright Ideas* graphic organizers.

The Lesson

1. Ask students what some of their favorite toys are, even ones they had when they were babies. Allow students to share their favorite toys with the class.

2. Then, explain to students that they will be describing their favorite toys in writing pieces. But first, they need to think of all of their favorite toys they could describe.

3. Give each student a *Bright Ideas* graphic organizer (page 24). Then, copy the sample graphic organizer (page 26) onto the *Bright Ideas Overhead*. Show students some of the toys mentioned on the sample, as well as how they will complete their own graphic organizers.

4. Allow students to complete their graphic organizers with partners, discussing different ideas as they create lists on their graphic organizers. Then, tell the class to circle the one toy on their graphic organizers that they wish to describe in their writing. Collect the graphic organizers for later use in the *A Shower of Words* drafting lesson (pages 41–42). You may also have students bring their favorite toys to class, so that they can refer to them in the drafting lesson.

ELL Support

Allow ELL students to look around the room for toys they might wish to describe if they cannot think of some of their own. This will help them form more ideas for their graphic organizers.

Extension Idea

Challenge students to create lists of toys they might describe under certain categories, such as stuffed toys or toys that move. You might also challenge them to invent their own toys that they could describe.

Connections to Other Lessons

Please refer to the following lessons to continue the steps in the process for creating *descriptive* writing pieces.

- *A Shower of Words*—pages 41–42
- *Look It Up*—pages 69–70
- *Lending a Hand*—pages 109–110
- *Share the Love*—pages 113–114

Name _____

Bright Ideas for Toys

Directions: Create a list of items you would like to describe on the light bulb below. Circle the item you want to write more about.

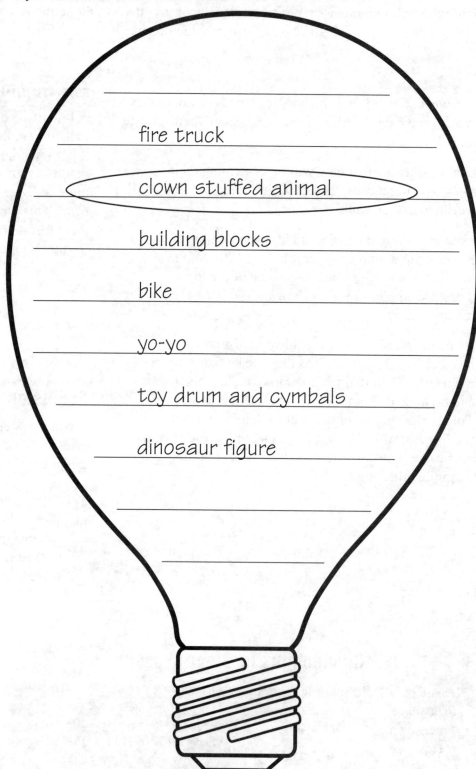

fire truck

clown stuffed animal

building blocks

bike

yo-yo

toy drum and cymbals

dinosaur figure

Stories to Tell Graphic Organizer

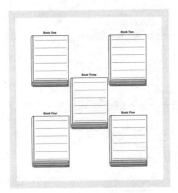

Skills Connection

Type of Writing— personal narratives

Prewriting— brainstorming ideas/making lists

Bloom's Level— Analysis (See page 8 for a description.)

Working with Young Students: Aid younger students as they search for topics to share by limiting their topics to one category, such as family holidays or family vacations. This will make it easier for them to decide which stories to share in their *narratives*.

Why Use the Graphic Organizer

- It is important that students identify themselves with their writings. The graphic organizer, *Stories to Tell,* allows students to lists major events in their lives that they could use in personal *narratives*.

How to Use the Graphic Organizer

1. Ask students if there are certain things they enjoy doing with family, friends, or by themselves. Are there any special events they enjoy attending? Display the *Stories to Tell Overhead*. Write the events and activities the students name on the overhead. Then, ask students if they have any stories to tell about the activities or events they listed. What did they do during those events?

2. Explain to the class that they will be writing stories about themselves, which tells others about things that have happened in their lives. Their stories can be about activities they have attended, their families, or any other stories about themselves.

3. Distribute the *Stories to Tell* graphic organizers (page 28) to the students. Then, allow them to complete their graphic organizers with ideas of stories they could tell about themselves. You may choose to refer to the sample graphic organizer (page 30) if students are having a difficult time brainstorming ideas for their own *narratives*.

4. Have students circle the story or event that they would like to write more about.

ELL Support

Allow ELL students to record their ideas on tape recorders. They can then work with partners to write the ideas on their graphic organizers, as their partners listen to their tape-recorded ideas.

Extension Idea

Encourage students to sketch pictures of the one event they circled on their graphic organizers. They should include the things that occurred during that event in their sketches. This way, students can get pictures in their minds of what they would like to tell in their *narratives*.

Name _____

Stories to Tell

Directions: Write ideas for stories you could tell about yourself on the books below. Circle the story you would like to write more about.

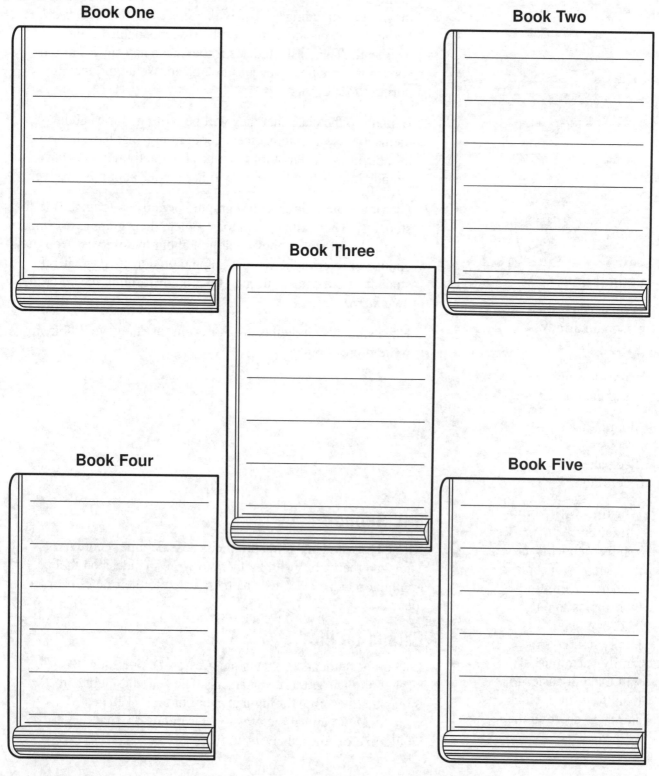

Book One

Book Two

Book Three

Book Four

Book Five

Family Moments to Tell

Standard/Objective

- **Prewriting:** Uses writing and other methods (making lists) to describe familiar person, places, objects, or experiences. (McREL Language Arts, 1.6)
- Students will brainstorm family memories that they could tell about in personal *narratives* on their *Stories to Tell* graphic organizers. They will then compare their ideas with those of their classmates to help one another decide on the topics for their *narratives*.

The Lesson

1. Share a story with the class about a holiday or vacation you have spent with your family. Explain to the students that we all have special memories of times we have spent with our families. We are now going to share those memories by writing stories about ourselves and our special family moments.

2. Distribute the *Stories to Tell* graphic organizer (page 28) to the students. Tell students to think of holidays, vacations, or other family memories they have. Then, tell them to write those ideas on their graphic organizers. You may choose to model this for students using the *Stories to Tell Overhead*.

3. Once students have completed their graphic organizers, ask them to find partners. Then, with their partners, have the students share their memories. Have their partners discuss which memory they feel is the most interesting on their peers' graphic organizers. Then, have each student choose his or her favorite memory to write about in the personal *narrative* and circle it on the graphic organizer.

4. Collect the students' graphic organizers so they can use them as they write their personal *narrative* drafts (see pages 49–50, *Along the Way*).

ELL Support

Allow ELL students to record their family memories on tape recorders. They can then work with partners to write the ideas on their graphic organizers, as their partners listen to the tape-recorded ideas.

Extension Idea

Encourage students to sketch pictures of the one family memory they circled on their graphic organizers on the back of their papers. This way, they can get pictures in their minds of what they would like to tell in their *narratives*.

Connections to Other Lessons

Please refer to the following lessons to continue the steps in the process for creating *narrative* writing pieces.

- *Along the Way*—pages 49–50
- *Mr. Fix It*—pages 73–74
- *Like a Sore Thumb*—pages 89–90
- *Memory Makers*—pages 121–122

Name _____

Stories to Tell for Family Memories

Directions: Write ideas for stories you could tell about yourself on the books below. Circle the story you would like to write more about.

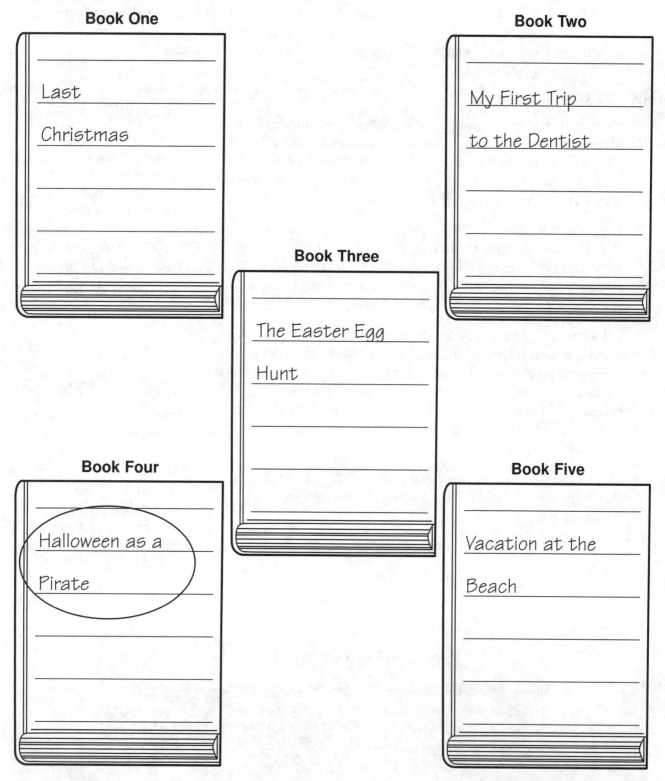

Book One

Last

Christmas

Book Two

My First Trip

to the Dentist

Book Three

The Easter Egg

Hunt

Book Four

Halloween as a

Pirate

Book Five

Vacation at the

Beach

Doorway to Drawings Graphic Organizer

Skills Connection

Type of Writing— picture books

Prewriting— creating illustrations to generate thought

Bloom's Level— Synthesis (See page 8 for a description.)

Working with Young Students: Give younger students literature books to look through as they create their own characters. Allow them to use the *picture books* as examples for the types of characters they might wish to include in their own *picture books*. You might also choose to discuss these characters as a class.

Why Use the Graphic Organizer

- It is often easier for students to create writings by first creating illustrations. *Doorway to Drawings* asks students to illustrate pictures to help brainstorm ideas for cartoon-like characters that they might use as they create *picture books*.

How to Use the Graphic Organizer

1. Show students various Dr. Seuss books, such as *The Cat in the Hat*, *Green Eggs and Ham*, or *The Lorax*. Then, ask them to name the characters in the books. What do they like about the characters? What makes them fun to read about? Have students name other characters they have read about or have seen on television.

2. Show students the *Doorway to Drawings Overhead*. Explain to them that they will use graphic organizers to create characters which could be used in their own *picture books*. They will draw various characters they would like to use in their stories on their graphic organizers.

3. Distribute the *Doorway to Drawings* graphic organizers (page 32) to the students. Then, have the class complete their organizers with characters they would like to use. Allow the students to color their characters as well, if they choose to do so.

ELL Support

Ask ELL students to cut out pictures from catalogs or computer graphics and paste them on their graphic organizers. They can then use these photos as their characters, rather than creating their own, if they choose to do so.

Extension Idea

Have students create characters by combining various attributes from characters that already exist, to create their original characters.

Name _____

Doorway to Drawings

Directions: Draw cartoon characters in the doors below. You will later use these characters in a picture book.

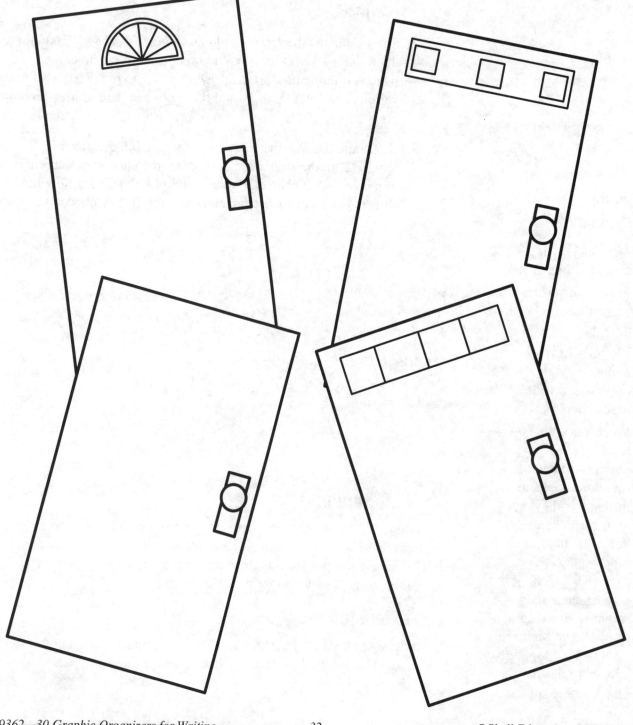

• •

Doorway to Family Drawings

Standard/Objective

- **Prewriting:** Uses prewriting strategies to plan written work (e.g., draws pictures to generate ideas). (McREL Language Arts, Standard 1.1)
- Students will generate ideas for original characters to be used in *picture books* by creating drawings of those possible characters on their *Doorway to Drawings* graphic organizers. They will also relate their characters to family members or friends in some way.

The Lesson

1. Read a *picture book* by Patricia Polacco to the class. Explain to the class that most of the stories written by this author were about her family members or friends. Ask the class what stories they could tell about family members or friends. *Have any of their friends or families done something unusual or traveled somewhere interesting? Do any of them stand out?*

2. Explain to the class that they will be creating *picture books* about their families or friends. However, they can choose to create funny characters to use in the books, rather than actual pictures of their friends and family.

3. Show students the sample graphic organizer (page 34). Explain to the class that they will be using their graphic organizers to draw the different characters they would like to use in their stories about their friends or families. However, they do not have to necessarily look like people. Distribute the *Doorway to Drawings* graphic organizers (page 32) for students to complete.

4. Then, collect the graphic organizers to be used later in the *Take Action* drafting lesson (pages 53–54).

ELL Support

Ask ELL students to cut out pictures from catalogues or computer graphics and paste them on their graphic organizers. They can then use these photos as their family or friend characters, rather than creating their own, if they choose to do so.

Extension Idea

Have students create characters by combining various attributes from many family members to create just one of their original family member characters. For example, one student might have a character that has blonde hair like the student's sister, but has a soccer ball in his hand, like the student's brother.

Connections to Other Lessons

Please refer to the following lessons to continue the steps in the process for creating *picture books*.

- *Take Action*—pages 53–54
- *Puzzle Pieces*—pages 81–82
- *The Strongest Word*—pages 93–94
- *Tell Me a Story*—pages 125–126

Name _____

Doorway to Drawings for Family Characters

Directions: Draw cartoon characters in the doors below. You will later use these characters in a picture book.

Art courtesy of Jaime Ortiz

Snapshots of Me Graphic Organizer

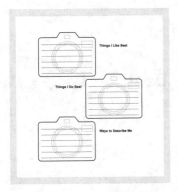

Skills Connection

Type of Writing— friendly letters

Prewriting—recording observations

Bloom's Level— Evaluation (See page 8 for a description.)

Working with Young Students: You may choose to allow younger students to work with partners as they complete their graphic organizers. This way, they can help one another with answering the questions about themselves.

Why Use the Graphic Organizer

- When students use *Snapshots of Me,* they evaluate themselves in order to create details for friendly letters. This evaluation promotes higher level thinking skills, which occur in the Evaluation level of Bloom's Taxonomy.
- The *Snapshots of Me* graphic organizer also allows students to state various observations to help them generate ideas for their *friendly letters*.

How to Use the Graphic Organizer

1. Ask the class if they have ever received letters in the mail. How does it make them feel when they get letters from loved ones? Explain to them that they will be writing their own *friendly letters* to people they know, but they must first decide what to write in their letters.

2. Place the *Snapshots of Me Overhead* so that students can see it. Then, complete the graphic organizer on the overhead, as if you are the one that will be writing the letter.

3. Distribute the *Snapshots of Me* graphic organizers (page 36) to the students. Then, ask them to complete their organizers, writing observations about themselves in each of the cameras. Tell them that they can use the information from their graphic organizers to write their own *friendly letters*.

ELL Support

Allow ELL students to work with partners when completing their graphic organizers. This way, they can get help with writing their answers.

Extension Idea

Challenge students to answer other questions on their organizers, such as "What are the most important things I have done in my life?" or "What can I do to help others?" This way, they are evaluating themselves even more.

Name _____

Snapshots of Me

Directions: Write the things you like best, the things you do best, and the way you would describe yourself on the cameras below.

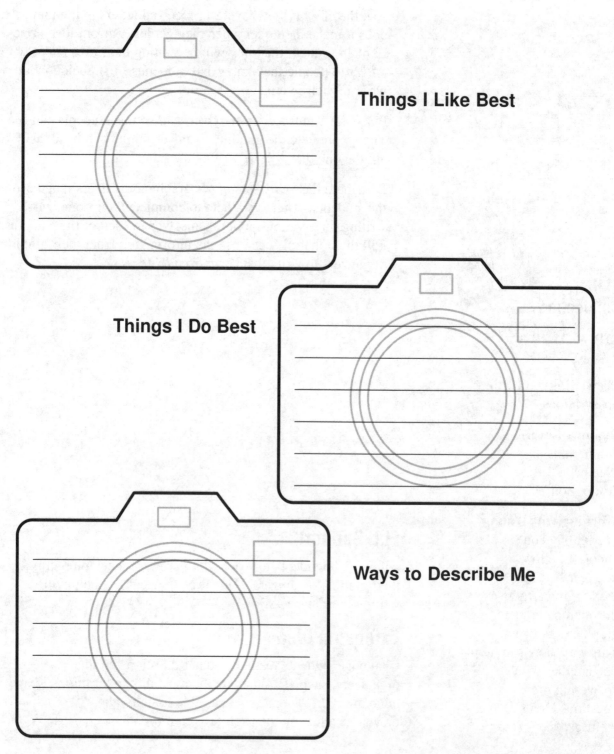

Things I Like Best

Things I Do Best

Ways to Describe Me

Sending Snapshots to Another Class

Standard/Objective

- **Prewriting:** Uses prewriting strategies to plan written work (e.g., records observations). (McREL Language Arts, Standard 1.1)

- Students will use their *Snapshots of Me* graphic organizers to evaluate themselves, by stating what they do best, what they like best, and writing descriptions of themselves. They will later use this information in *friendly letters* to students in other classrooms.

The Lesson

1. Before beginning this activity, set up a *friendly letter* exchange with another class. Arrange it so that students can be assigned to other students in another classroom. Once the writing process for creating a *friendly letter* is completed, then students can exchange their letters with the students in the other class. You may wish to continue the letter exchange throughout the entire school year or strictly for this activity only.

2. Explain to the students that they will be writing letters to other students in the school. These students will be their pen pals. But first, they need to decide what they will say in their *friendly letters* to the other students.

3. Distribute the *Snapshots of Me* graphic organizers (page 36) to the students. Then, explain to them how to complete their graphic organizers. You may wish to show them the sample graphic organizer (page 38) as an example.

4. Once students have completed their graphic organizers, collect them for use in the drafting lesson, *Building a Letter* (pages 61–62). Then, assign each student a pen pal from the other classroom. You may wish to tell them their pen pals' first and last names, or only their first names. Or, you may wish to only tell each student if he/she will be writing to a boy or a girl.

ELL Support

Allow ELL students to work with partners when completing their graphic organizers for their student pen pals. This way, they can get help with writing their answers.

Extension Idea

Challenge students to answer other questions on their organizers, such as "What are the most important things I have done in my life?" or "What can I do to help others?" This way, they are evaluating themselves even more, as they begin the writing process for creating *friendly letters* to other students.

Connections to Other Lessons

Please refer to the following lessons to continue the steps in the process for creating *friendly letters*.

- *Building a Letter*—pages 61–62
- *The Name Game*—pages 65–66
- *Vegetable Variety*—pages 97–98
- *In the Mail*—pages 117–118

Name _____

Snapshots of Me for Pen Pal Writing

Directions: Write the things you like best, the things you do best, and the way you would describe yourself on the cameras below.

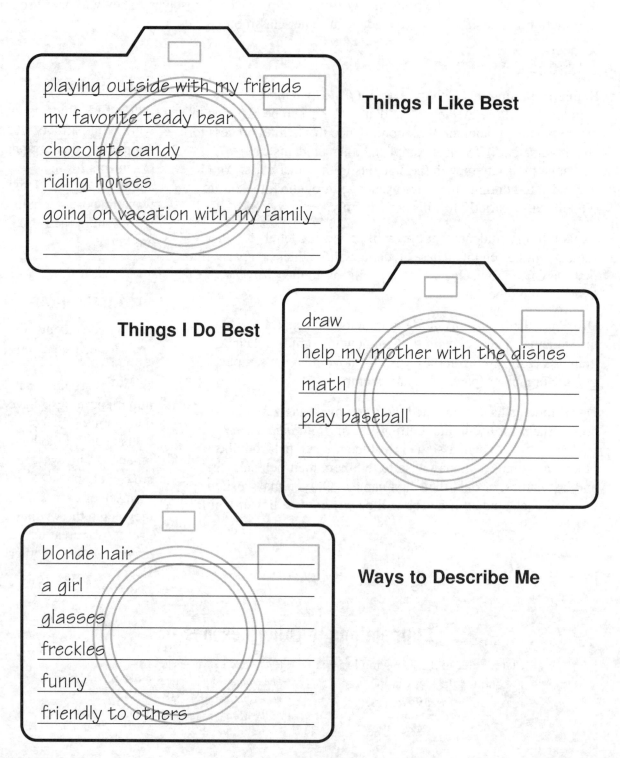

Things I Like Best

playing outside with my friends
my favorite teddy bear
chocolate candy
riding horses
going on vacation with my family

Things I Do Best

draw
help my mother with the dishes
math
play baseball

Ways to Describe Me

blonde hair
a girl
glasses
freckles
funny
friendly to others

A Shower of Words Graphic Organizer

Skills Connection

Type of Writing— descriptive

Drafting—listing descriptive words

Bloom's Level— Knowledge (See page 7 for a description.)

Working with Young Students: To help younger students better understand descriptive words, allow them to hold objects you have given to them. Then, let them take turns describing their objects. Write the adjectives they use on the *A Shower of Words Overhead,* which can then be used as an example.

Why Use the Graphic Organizer

- Students often use the same common descriptive words in their writings. The *A Shower of Words* graphic organizer asks students to list adjectives that could be used to describe objects. By completing the organizer, students will have lists of adjectives to refer to when writing, so that their writings will be more vivid.

How to Use the Graphic Organizer

1. Show students a stuffed animal. Ask them what words they would use to describe the animal. As students list adjectives they would use to describe the animal, record them on the *A Shower of Words Overhead.* You may wish to call these words either adjectives or descriptive words.

2. Distribute the *A Shower of Words* graphic organizers (page 40) to the students. Explain to them that they are now going to describe objects they have interest in, such as their favorite toys.

3. After students have described their objects using adjectives on their graphic organizers, ask them to create at least three sentences about their objects, using the adjectives they listed, at the bottom of their graphic organizers. You may choose to model how to create the sentences for your students using the *A Shower of Words Overhead.*

ELL Support

Have dictionaries readily available for the ELL students. This way, they can find any words that they are struggling to use or spell in their drafts.

Extension Idea

Encourage students to use vivid adjectives. Have them use thesauruses to form stronger words.

Name _____

A Shower of Words

Directions: Pick an object. Think of words to describe your object. Then, list the words on the umbrella. Use the lines at the bottom of the page to write at least two complete sentences about your object.

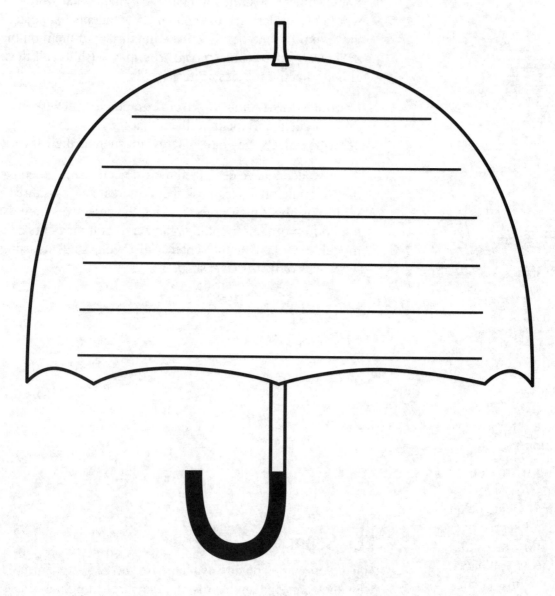

_____

_____

_____

_____

A Shower of Toys

Standard/Objective

- **Drafting:** Uses adjectives in written compositions (e.g., uses descriptive words). (McREL Language Arts, Standard 3.5)
- Students will create lists of adjectives they could use to describe their favorite toys. They will then use those lists in *descriptive* writing pieces.

The Lesson

1. Bring in a toy to share with the class. Ask the class what words they might use to describe the toy. Write their adjectives on the *A Shower of Words Overhead*.

2. Next, distribute the *Bright Ideas* graphic organizers (page 24) that students completed in the pre-writing activity. Tell students that they will now be writing adjectives or describing words that they could use to tell about their favorite toys. Give each student *A Shower of Words* graphic organizer (page 40). Ask them to complete their graphic organizers, describing their favorite toys.

3. Once students have listed their adjectives, model how to create a draft to describe the toy you brought to class. The draft should include the words listed on the overhead. You may also show students the sample graphic organizer (page 42) if they need more examples of how to use their descriptive words in sentences.

4. Ask the class to now use the lines on the bottom of their graphic organizers to create at least three sentences to describe their favorite toys. Once students have completed their paragraphs, collect their drafts so that they can be used in the *Look It Up* lesson (pages 69–70).

ELL Support

Have dictionaries readily available for the ELL students. This way, they can find any words that they are struggling to use or spell in their toy *descriptive* drafts.

Extension Idea

Encourage students to use vivid adjectives when describing their favorite toys. Have them use thesauruses to form stronger words.

Connections to Other Lessons

Please refer to the following lessons to continue the steps in the process for creating *descriptive* writing pieces.

- *Look It Up*—pages 69–70
- *Lending a Hand*—pages 109–110
- *Share the Love*—pages 113–114

Name _____

A Shower of Words for Toys

Directions: Pick an object. Think of words to describe your object. Then, list the words on the umbrella. Use the lines at the bottom of the page to write at least two complete sentences about your object.

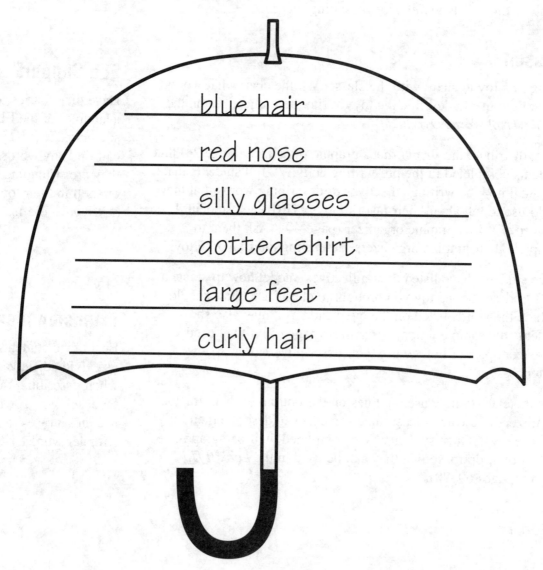

blue hair

red nose

silly glasses

dotted shirt

large feet

curly hair

My favorite toy is Funny the Clown. She has blue hair and a red nose.

My clown wears silly glasses and a shirt with dots. Funny has large feet and curly hair.

Words from the Wise Graphic Organizer

Why Use the Graphic Organizer

- The *Words from the Wise* graphic organizer helps students organize their thoughts as they record information they know about given topics. It then allows them to turn that information into paragraphs or drafts.

How to Use the Graphic Organizer

1. Read an *informational* nonfiction book to the class. Then, place the *Words from the Wise Overhead* so that students can see it. Ask the class to tell you everything they learned about the topic in the book. Write their stated facts on the first owl of the organizer.

2. Then, tell students that you are now going to turn their facts into a paragraph. Rewrite the facts in paragraph form on the second owl. Tell the students that you have now created an *informational* rough draft.

3. Give each student a copy of the *Words from the Wise* graphic organizer (page 44). Ask the students to choose one item that they would like to tell others about in *informational* drafts. Have them then write the things they know about the items they chose on their *Words from the Wise* graphic organizers. Once they have recorded all of their facts, have them complete their drafts as well.

Skills Connection

Type of Writing— informational

Drafting—recording information

Bloom's Level— Comprehension (See page 7 for a description.)

Working with Young Students: Allow younger students to work in small groups as they write their drafts. This way, they can help one another with facts to use in their drafts.

ELL Support

Have ELL students record their facts on tape recorders. They can then transfer those facts onto their rough drafts, rather than having to struggle with writing the facts twice on their graphic organizers.

Extension Idea

Allow students to do further research on their topics. Have them record the information they find during their research on their graphic organizers. Then, ask them to use that information in their drafts, along with the information they already knew about their topics.

Name _____

Words from the Wise

Directions: Write everything you know about your topic in the first owl. Then, turn those sentences into a paragraph in the second owl.

Wise Science Words

Standard/Objective

- **Drafting:** Writes in a variety of forms or genres (e.g., information pieces). (McREL Language Arts, Standard 1.7)
- Students will write facts concerning science topics about which they are experts using their *Words from the Wise* graphic organizers. They will then use those facts to write drafts about their topics.

The Lesson

1. Display the *Words from the Wise Overhead*. Then, copy the information from the sample graphic organizer (page 46) concerning the four seasons onto the overhead. Ask the class if there is other information they know about the four seasons that could be added to the first owl. Then, show them how the facts can be made into an *informational* paragraph using the second owl on the overhead.

2. Give students their completed *Shopping for Ideas* graphic organizers (page 16), on which they chose science topics for their informational drafts. Tell them that they are now going to create their own science drafts using facts they know about their chosen science topics.

3. Give each student a copy of the *Words from the Wise* graphic organizers (page 44). Ask them to complete their organizers just as you previously showed them. Once students have listed the facts they know about their science topics on their graphic organizers, have them create their drafts as well on their organizers.

4. Collect the drafts so that students can use them in the editing lesson, *At the End of the Rope* (pages 77–78).

ELL Support

Have ELL students record their science facts on tape recorders. They can then transfer those facts onto their rough drafts, rather than having to struggle with writing the facts twice on their graphic organizers.

Extension Idea

Allow students to do further research on their science topics. Have them record the information they find during their research on their graphic organizers. Then, ask them to use that information in their science *informational* drafts, along with the information they already knew.

Connections to Other Lessons

Please refer to the following lessons to continue the steps in the process for creating *informational* writing pieces.

- *At the End of the Rope*—pages 77–78
- *One More Time*—pages 101–102
- *Picture This*—pages 133–134

Name _____

Words from the Wise for the Four Seasons Science Topic

Directions: Write everything you know about your topic in the first owl. Then, turn those sentences into a paragraph in the second owl.

Fall is called autumn.

Summer is hot. Trees get

leaves in the spring and lose

them in the fall. Winter is cold.

The trees do not have leaves.

The four seasons are spring, summer, fall, and winter. In the spring, the trees get their leaves. Then, summer comes. The weather is hot. Next, we have fall or autumn. The trees lose their leaves. When winter arrives, it is cold. There are no leaves on the trees.

Along the Way Graphic Organizer

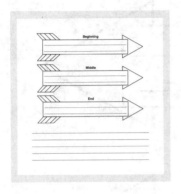

Why Use the Graphic Organizer

- Putting events in sequential order is essential when writing narratives. The *Along the Way* graphic organizer provides the necessary structure so that students can write the events of their personal experiences in sequential order. They can then refer to their graphic organizers to create *narrative* drafts.

How to Use the Graphic Organizer

1. Have students compose a list of special events in their lives. Then, ask them to look at the lists they created. What events did they want to include in their *narratives*? Allow them to share some of their events with the class.

2. Display the *Along the Way Overhead*. Explain to students that they will now write about one of their events. But first, they must write the things that took place during their events in sequential order. Explain to the class what it means to write in sequential order. You may also choose to read several picture books and ask the class what happened in the story, from the first major event to the last. Model how to write items in sequential order using the overhead. You may use an event that has taken place in your own life as an example.

3. Give each student a copy of the *Along the Way* graphic organizer (page 48). Then, ask each student to write about the major event in his or her life, recording what happened from beginning to end in sequential order on the graphic organizer. Once students have recorded the main events on their organizers, have them write those events in paragraph form, creating *narrative* drafts, using the lines provided on the bottom of their graphic organizers.

ELL Support

If it is helpful for ELL students to draw pictures of their major events, and then have other higher level students or teacher's aides record what is occurring in the pictures, allow them to do so on their organizers. The ELL students can then write their own *narratives*, using the captions from their pictures as guides.

Extension Idea

Encourage students to add details to their sequence of events to make their writings vivid and exciting.

Name _____

Along the Way

Directions: Write the main events for your narrative in the arrows. Write what happened at the beginning, the middle, and the end. At the bottom of the page, write your narrative paragraph.

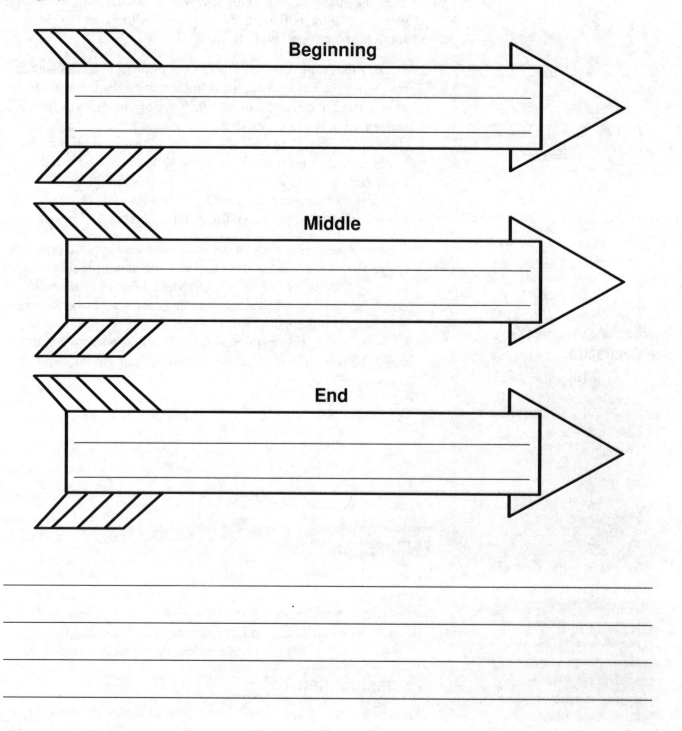

Beginning

Middle

End

_____

_____

_____

_____

• •

Along the Way to Family Memories

Standard/Objective

- **Drafting:** Uses strategies to organize written work (e.g., uses a sequence of events). (McREL Language Arts, Standard 1.5)

- Students will use their *Along the Way* graphic organizers to record the beginning, middle, and end of the main events in their family memories. They will then create *narrative* drafts using the events recorded on their graphic organizers.

The Lesson

1. Read the book *We Had a Picnic This Sunday Past* by Jacqueline Woodson to the students. Then, tell the class that this is a narrative of a girl telling about her family reunion. Place the *Along the Way Overhead* so that students can easily see it. Then, ask students what major events happened at the beginning, middle, and end of the story. Write their thoughts on the overhead.

2. Give students their completed prewriting lessons, *Stories to Tell* (page 28). Ask them to review the different topics they chose to include in their *narratives*. Allow them to share some of their ideas with the class. Then, distribute the *Along the Way* graphic organizers (page 48).

3. Have students complete their organizers for one of their family memories, writing their events in sequential order. Then, show them the sample organizer (page 50). You may wish to rewrite the sample graphic organizer onto the overhead. Explain to the students that they are now going to create *narrative* drafts using the events on their graphic organizers, as shown on the sample graphic organizer. Have them create their drafts using the lines provided on their graphic organizers.

4. Allow students to complete their organizers and write their *narrative* drafts. Collect the drafts so that they can be used in the *Mr. Fix-It* editing lesson (pages 73–74).

ELL Support

If it is helpful for ELL students to draw pictures of their family memories, and then have higher level students or teacher's aides record what is occurring in the pictures, allow them to do so on their organizers. The ELL students can then write their own family memory *narratives*, using the captions from their pictures as guides.

Extension Idea

Encourage students to add details to their sequence of events to make their family memories more vivid and exciting.

Connections to Other Lessons

Please refer to the following lessons to continue the steps in the process for creating *narrative* writing pieces.

- *Mr. Fix It*—pages 73–74
- *Like a Sore Thumb*—pages 89–90
- *Memory Makers*—pages 121–122

Name _____

Along the Way for Family Memories

Directions: Write the main events for your narrative in the arrows. Write what happened at the beginning, the middle, and the end. At the bottom of the page, write your narrative paragraph.

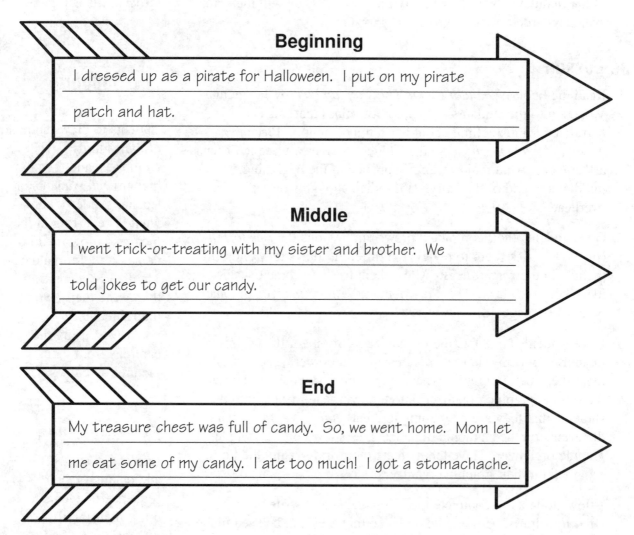

Beginning

I dressed up as a pirate for Halloween. I put on my pirate patch and hat.

Middle

I went trick-or-treating with my sister and brother. We told jokes to get our candy.

End

My treasure chest was full of candy. So, we went home. Mom let me eat some of my candy. I ate too much! I got a stomachache.

Draft:

For Halloween this year, I dressed up like a pirate. I put on a pirate patch and a pirate hat. Then, I went trick-or-treating with my brother and sister. We told jokes to get our candy. My treasure chest soon became full of candy. So, we went home. Mom let me eat some of my candy. I ate too much! I got a stomachache.

Take Action Graphic Organizer

Skills Connection

Type of Writing— picture books

Drafting—identify problem and solution

Bloom's Level— Analysis (See page 8 for a description.)

Working with Young Students: If you feel that younger students will have a difficult time creating problems on their own, you may choose to write problems on small pieces of paper. Then, allow each student to randomly choose a problem you created that he/she can use in his or her story.

Why Use the Graphic Organizer

- Students must realize that all problems can have solutions. The *Take Action* graphic organizer allows students to create problems and solutions that can be used in their *picture books*.

How to Use the Graphic Organizer

1. Read a *picture book* to the class, such as *Thank You, Mr. Falker* by Patricia Polacco. Then, tell the class that most stories have problems, or events, that occur, which the main characters must solve. What was the problem in the story? What was the solution?

2. Place the *Take Action Overhead* where students can see it. Write the problem and solution from the story on the overhead. Then, students must decide what problems their characters will face, as well as how they will solve their problems.

3. Distribute the *Take Action* graphic organizers (page 52) to the students. Tell students that they need to think of problems that could occur in their stories and record them on their graphic organizers. They also need to think about how their characters will solve those problems. They should record those solutions on their organizers as well.

4. After students have created their problems and solutions, have them write their *picture book* drafts on the back of their graphic organizers or on other sheets of paper.

ELL Support

Allow ELL students to work with partners or teacher's aides when creating their rough drafts.

Extension Idea

Encourage students to create layouts of their *picture books* as they write their drafts. Ask them to include page numbers and divide their drafts into those separate pages.

Name _____

Take Action

Directions: Write the problem of your story in the lines below. Write the solution in the movie projector.

Problem

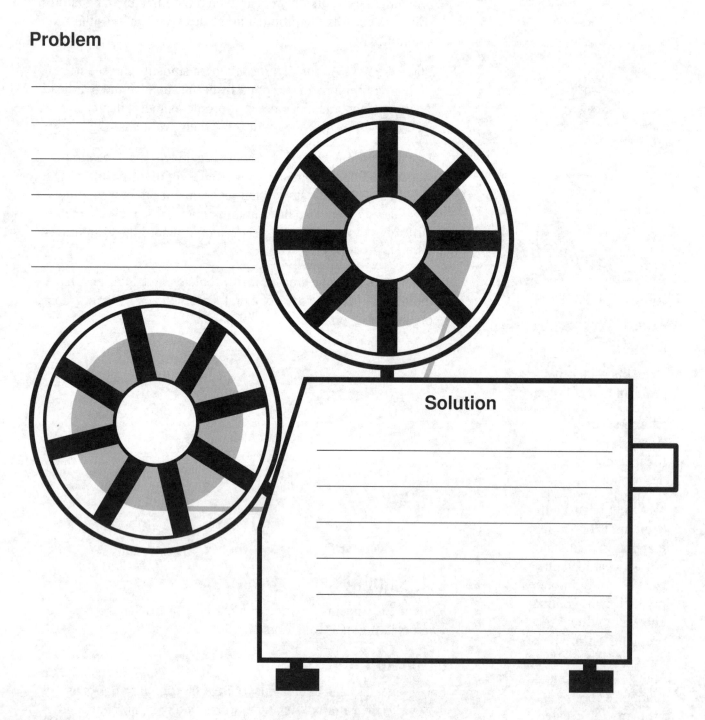

Solution

Take Family Action

Standard/Objective

- **Drafting:** Knows setting, main characters, main events, sequence, and problems in stories. (McREL Language Arts, Standard 6.3)

- Students will use their *Take Action* graphic organizers to create problems and solutions that they will use in their *picture book* drafts.

The Lesson

1. Read *Pigs Will Be Pigs* by Amy Axelrod to the class. Then, ask them what major problem the pig family faced. Write the problem on the *Take Action Overhead*. Next, ask the class how the family solved their problem. Write the solution on the overhead as well.

2. Tell the students that they will be using their family characters that that they created in the prewriting lesson, *Doorway to Drawings,* in *picture books*. But, what problems might your families face? How will they solve those problems? Show students the sample graphic organizer (page 54), which has an example of a problem and several solutions to that problem. You may also choose to read more *picture books*, so that students can have more practice identifying problems and solutions.

3. Next, distribute the *Take Action* graphic organizers (page 52) to the students, as well as the completed *Doorway to Drawings* graphic organizers (page 32). Allow students to work in groups to brainstorm possible problems and solutions that they can use in their stories. Have them record their ideas on their graphic organizers. They may choose to think of silly dilemmas that their families have faced to use in their *picture books*, such as where to go on vacation or what to eat for dinner.

4. Then, ask the class to create rough drafts using one of the problems from their graphic organizers. You may wish to show students how to write their rough drafts, adding fun twists and turns to make their stories entertaining.

5. Once students have completed their drafts, collect them so that they can later be used in the *Puzzle Pieces* editing lesson (pages 81–82).

ELL Support

Allow ELL students to work with partners or teacher's aides when creating their family *picture book* rough drafts.

Extension Idea

Encourage students to create layouts of their family-related *picture books* as they write their drafts. Ask them to include page numbers and divide their drafts into those separate pages.

Connections to Other Lessons

Please refer to the following lessons to continue the steps in the process for creating *picture books*.

- *Puzzle Pieces*—pages 81–82
- *The Strongest Word*—pages 93–94
- *Tell Me a Story*—pages 125–126

Name _____

Take Action for Family Picture Books

Directions: Write the problem of your story in the lines below. Write the solution in the movie projector.

Problem

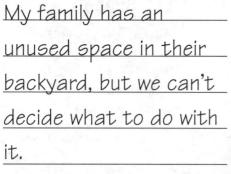

My family has an
unused space in their
backyard, but we can't
decide what to do with
_it._

Solution

Build a swing set

Create a sandbox

Plant a garden

Poetry in Motion Graphic Organizer

Skills Connection

Type of Writing— poetry

Drafting—creating a poem

Bloom's Level— Synthesis (See page 8 for a description.)

Working with Young Students: Younger students might benefit by creating several rhyming poems together as a class before creating their own poems.

Why Use the Graphic Organizer

- Often, the most difficult part of writing poetry is organizing the writing. The *Poetry in Motion* graphic organizer is an organizational tool that allows students to create poems by writing rhyming lines that can be combined to form the poems.

How to Use the Graphic Organizer

1. Read several nursery rhymes or other rhyming poems to the class. Then, write some of the nursery rhymes on the board. Leave blanks in the place of several of the rhyming words. Ask the class to replace the blanks with various words that rhyme. Tell the class that after they create sentences that rhyme, they can then combine those sentences to create poems.

2. Place the *Poetry in Motion Overhead* where students can see it. Ask for a volunteer to list two rhyming words. Then, as a class, create a line of poetry using the two rhyming words in the first truck on the overhead. Do the same with two more sets of rhyming words. Tell the class that the poem should be about one topic.

3. Distribute the *Poetry in Motion* graphic organizers (page 56) to the students. Allow them to work in groups to create poems. Remind the class that each person needs to create his or her own poem, but that group members can help form lines if some "inspiration" is needed.

4. Next, use the overhead to show students how they can now combine their lines to create poems. Have them do this on the back of their graphic organizers.

ELL Support

Allow ELL students to work with higher-level partners when writing their drafts. This way, the higher-level students can check the ELL students' poems, to make sure that they flow and that the correct words were used.

Extension Idea

Challenge students to create rhyming poems that have more than three lines. They can simply add more lines on the back of their graphic organizers.

Name _____

Poetry in Motion

Directions: Choose two rhyming words. Write those words on the front of the first truck. On the back of the truck, write a line of poetry that rhymes. You have to use the two rhyming words you chose! Do the same on the other trucks, using more rhyming pairs.

Animals in Motion

Standard/Objective

- **Drafting:** Writes in a variety of forms or genres (e.g., poems). (McREL Language Arts, Standard 1.7)
- Students will use their *Poetry in Motion* graphic organizers to create lines about animals using rhyming words. They will then use those lines to create poems.

The Lesson

1. Read several rhyming poems about animals to the class. The literature book, *The Beauty of the Beast: Poems from the Animal Kingdom*, selected by Jack Prelutsky, contains animal *poetry*.

2. Ask the students to identify several of the words that rhymed from the poems. Explain to them that they are now going to be using their words from their *The Rhyme Climb* graphic organizers (page 20) to create their own animal poems. Show the class the sample graphic organizer (page 58) to give them ideas of how they will be creating their poems. Also remind students that they are not limited to using only those words listed on *The Rhyme Climb* graphic organizers.

3. Give each student a copy of the *Poetry in Motion* graphic organizer (page 56). Also, distribute their completed *The Rhyme Climb* graphic organizers. Ask students to complete their *Poetry in Motion* graphic organizers, using the rhyming words they developed in the previous lesson. Then, ask them to combine those lines to create their own poems.

4. After students have written their drafts, collect them so that they can be used in the editing lesson, *At the Car Wash* (pages 85–86).

ELL Support

Allow ELL students to work with higher level partners when writing their animal drafts. This way, the higher level students can check the ELL students' poems, to make sure that they flow and that the correct words were used.

Extension Idea

Challenge students to create animal poems that have more than three lines. They can simply add more lines on the back of their graphic organizers.

Connections to Other Lessons

Please refer to the following lessons to continue the steps in the process for creating *poetry*.

- *At the Car Wash*—pages 85–86
- *Ask Me Anything*—pages 105–106
- *Having a Ball*—pages 129–130

Name _____

Poetry in Motion for Animal Poems

Directions: Choose two rhyming words. Write those words on the front of the first truck. On the back of the truck, write a line of poetry that rhymes. You have to use the two rhyming words you chose!. Do the same on the other trucks, using more rhyming pairs.

Lee
bee

There once was a bee named Lee.

tree
fee

Who paid a small fee to live in a tree.

free
see

Though the tree wasn't free, it made him happy, you see.

Building a Letter Graphic Organizer

Skills Connection

Type of Writing— friendly letters

Drafting—parts of a letter

Bloom's Level— Evaluation (See page 8 for a description.)

Working with Young Students: It might be beneficial to younger students if you concentrate on only one part of the *friendly letter* a day. Have students write their greetings the first day, their bodies the second and third days, and their closings the fourth.

Why Use the Graphic Organizer

- The *Building a Letter* graphic organizer allows students to organize their *friendly letters* into three main sections: the greeting, body, and closing.

How to Use the Graphic Organizer

1. Read a *friendly letter* to the students. Then, display the *Building a Letter Overhead*. Point out to the students that there are three parts to a *friendly letter*: a greeting, a body, and a closing. Read the letter to the students once again. Then, ask them to identify the parts of the letter. Write those parts on the overhead. Discuss the use of commas after the greeting and closing of the letter.

2. Distribute the *Building a Letter* graphic organizer (page 60). Explain to students that they are now going to use their ideas to write *friendly letters* on their *Building a Letter* graphic organizers. But first, discuss with students possible greetings and closings they could use in their letters. Write their ideas on the overhead as well.

3. Allow students to create the three parts of their letters using their graphic organizers. Then, ask them to write their actual *friendly letter* drafts on separate sheets of paper, or allow them to use their graphic organizers as their drafts.

ELL Support

Provide ELL students with several examples of *friendly letters*. Allow them to refer to those letters for possible spellings and ideas as they write their *friendly letters*.

Extension Idea

Challenge students to think of creative greetings and closings that were not mentioned in class, which they could use in their *friendly letters*.

Name _____

Building a Letter

Directions: Write the greeting, body, and closing of your letter in the building below.

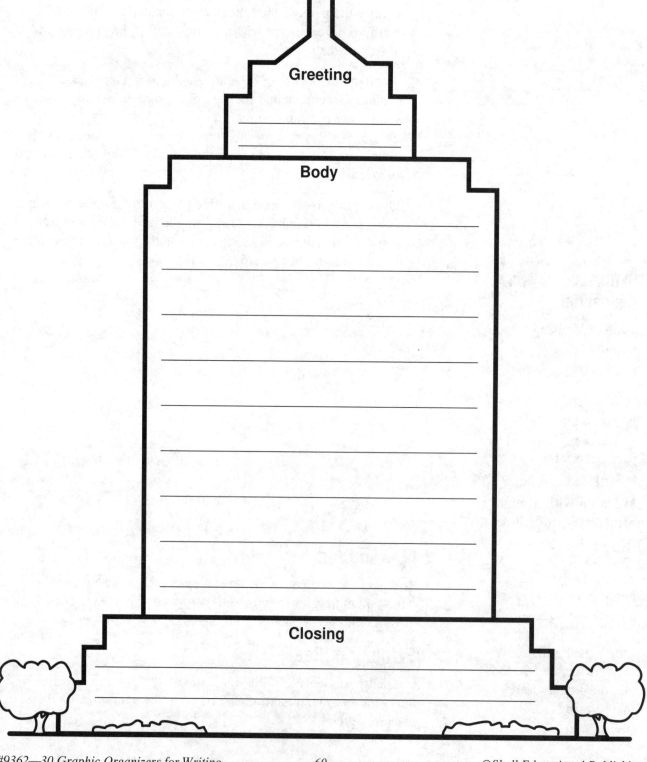

Greeting

Body

Closing

● ●

Building a Pen Pal Letter

Standard/Objective

- **Drafting:** Writes in a variety of forms or genres (friendly letters). (McREL Language Arts, Standard 1.7)
- Students will create pen pal *friendly letters* using their *Building a Letter* graphic organizers. They will then discuss the most difficult parts of a *friendly letter* to write, as well as the easiest, in small groups.

The Lesson

1. Prior to class, copy the sample graphic organizer (page 62) onto the *Building a Letter Overhead*. Then, read the letter to the class. Explain to the students the three parts of a *friendly letter*, as well as the rules for indenting and using commas when writing a *friendly letter*.

2. Give each student a copy of the *Building a Letter* graphic organizer (page 60). Then, give them their completed *Snapshots of Me* graphic organizers. Explain to the class that they are now going to write their own friendly letters to their pen pals. They will create greetings, bodies, and closings using their graphic organizers. Tell the class that they should use the information they brainstormed on their *Snapshots of Me* graphic organizers (page 36) in the body of their letters.

3. Once the students have completed the rough drafts of their *friendly letters*, collect them so that they can be used in the editing lesson, *The Name Game* (pages 65–66). Then, divide the class into small groups. In their groups, ask the class to discuss the easiest part of writing a *friendly letter*, the most difficult part, and the part they liked writing best. Have them explain why they feel this way to their group members.

ELL Support

Provide ELL students with several examples of *friendly letters*. Allow them to refer to those letters for possible spellings and ideas as they write their pen pal *friendly letters*.

Extension Idea

Challenge students to think of creative greetings and closings that were not mentioned in class, which they could use in their pen pal *friendly letters*.

Connections to Other Lessons

Please refer to the following lessons to continue the steps in the process for creating *friendly letters*.

- *The Name Game*—pages 65–66
- *Vegetable Variety*—pages 97–98
- *In the Mail*—pages 117–118

Name _____

Building a Letter for Pen Pals

Directions: Write the greeting, body, and closing of your letter in the building below.

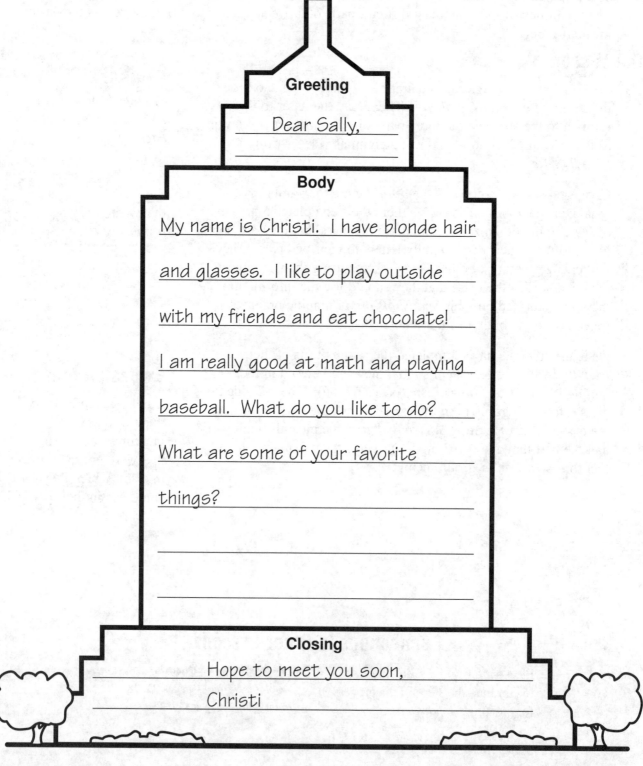

Greeting

Dear Sally,

Body

My name is Christi. I have blonde hair

and glasses. I like to play outside

with my friends and eat chocolate!

I am really good at math and playing

baseball. What do you like to do?

What are some of your favorite

things?

Closing

Hope to meet you soon,

Christi

The Name Game Graphic Organizer

Skills Connection

Type of Writing— friendly letters

Editing—capitalization of names and places

Bloom's Level— Knowledge (See page 7 for a description.)

Working with Young Students: Allow younger students to use only first names with the activity, rather than first and last names. You may also do the "places" portion as a class.

Why Use the Graphic Organizer

- Students are often familiar with capitalizing their own names, but they often do not capitalize the names of other people and places in their writings. *The Name Game* graphic organizer allows students to practice capitalizing names and places.

How to Use the Graphic Organizer

1. Write your name on the board. Then, write several of your students' names on the board as well. Ask the class what is important, or special, about writing names. Tell them that we always capitalize the names of people. Then, ask the class to name places they have lived or visited. Write the names of the places on the board. Explain that we also capitalize the names of cities and states as well.

2. Distribute *The Name Game* graphic organizers (page 64) to the students. Also display *The Name Game Overhead*. Tell students that they are now going to practice capitalizing names of people and places. Have the students go around the room, talking with other classmates. They should then write their classmates' first and last names on their graphic organizers, as well as their classmates' favorite places to visit. They need to pay special attention to capitalizing the names and places correctly. Model this for students using the overhead.

3. Then, have each student write *friendly letter* rough drafts. Tell students that they will need to look over their drafts, checking that they capitalized the names and places. Have them edit their drafts, making any corrections that are necessary.

ELL Support

Ask ELL students to work with partners when editing their friendly letter rough drafts. Allow them to help one another in finding the names and places in their *friendly letters*.

Extension Idea

Encourage students to add more proper nouns to their letters to make them more specific. Ask them to add the date, using the proper nouns correctly.

Name _____

The Name Game

Directions: Write names of people, cities, states, or countries in the boxes on the game board. Use correct capitalization.

The First and Last Name Game

Standard/Objective

- **Editing:** Uses conventions of capitalization in written compositions (e.g., first and last names). (McREL Language Arts, Standard 3.8)
- Students will use their *The Name Game* graphic organizers to practice writing first and last names of people they know, using correct capitalization. They will then edit their pen pal *friendly letters*, making sure that the names are capitalized correctly.

The Lesson

1. Distribute *The Name Game* graphic organizers (page 64) to the students. Tell students that since we have been writing letters to pen pals, we need to make sure that when we write their names, we always capitalize them.

2. Show students the sample graphic organizer (page 66). You may also choose to copy the information from the sample graphic organizer onto *The Name Game Overhead* prior to the lesson. Explain to students that they are now going to practice writing first and last names, using their graphic organizers. Have them write the first and last names of people they know on their graphic organizers, making sure they capitalize the names correctly. You may have students write the first names on the left side of their game boards, and the last names on the right side, as it is done on the sample graphic organizer.

3. Give students their pen pal *friendly letter* rough drafts. Ask the students to edit their *friendly letters*, making sure that they capitalized their pen pals first and last names. Collect their drafts so that they can be used in the revising activity, *Vegetable Variety* (pages 97-98).

ELL Support

Ask ELL students to work with partners when editing their pen pal *friendly letter* rough drafts. Allow them to help one another in finding the proper nouns in their *friendly letters*.

Extension Idea

Encourage students to add more proper nouns to their pen pal letters to make them more specific. Ask them to add the date, if they have not already done so, using the proper nouns correctly.

Connections to Other Lessons

Please refer to the following lessons to continue the steps in the process for creating *friendly letters*.

- *Vegetable Variety*—pages 97–98
- *In the Mail*—pages 117–118

Name _____

The Name Game for First and Last Names of People

Directions: Write names of people, cities, states, or countries in the boxes on the game board. Use correct capitalization.

	Christi		Parker		Heflin
Katie		Bryce		Roberts	
	Brendan		Scott		McCoy
Tom		Charles		Smith	
	Wade		Sorrell		Hodge
Sam		Melanie		Wicks	

Look It Up Graphic Organizer

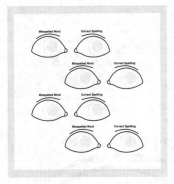

Skills Connection

Type of Writing— descriptive

Editing— using a dictionary

Bloom's Level— Comprehension (See page 7 for a description.)

Working with Young Students: Allow younger students to use picture dictionaries to help them find misspelled words in their writings.

Why Use the Graphic Organizer

- The *Look It Up* graphic organizer allows students to compare misspelled words to their correct spellings. By seeing the two words side by side on their organizers, the students can more easily compare and identify the misspelled words in their writing pieces.

How to Use the Graphic Organizer

1. Give each student a dictionary. Then, write a sentence on the board, misspelling one of the words. Ask the students to identify the misspelled word. Then, ask them to find the correct spelling using their dictionaries.

2. Next, place the *Look It Up Overhead* where students can see it. Write the misspelled word in the first eye. Then, ask for a volunteer to write the word correctly in the second eye. Ask the class if, by looking at the two words next to one another, they can more easily see which word is correctly spelled.

3. Give each student a copy of the *Look It Up* graphic organizer (page 68). Also, distribute previous writing drafts that students have written. Tell students that they are now going to edit their drafts, looking for any misspelled words. As they find the misspelled words, they should circle them, and then write the misspelled words on their graphic organizers. Students will then need to use their dictionaries to write the correct spellings on their organizers, as well as on their drafts. If you feel students will have a difficult time finding their own misspelled words, you may choose to proofread their drafts ahead of time, circling the misspelled words for them.

ELL Support

Allow ELL students to work with partners when editing their drafts. Ask their partners to help them find the misspelled words in their dictionaries.

Extension Idea

If students finish early, allow them to help other classmates find their misspelled words in their writing pieces, so that they will be sure to catch them all.

Name _____

Look It Up

Directions: Write the misspelled words from your draft in the first eye below. Then, write the correct spelling in the second eye.

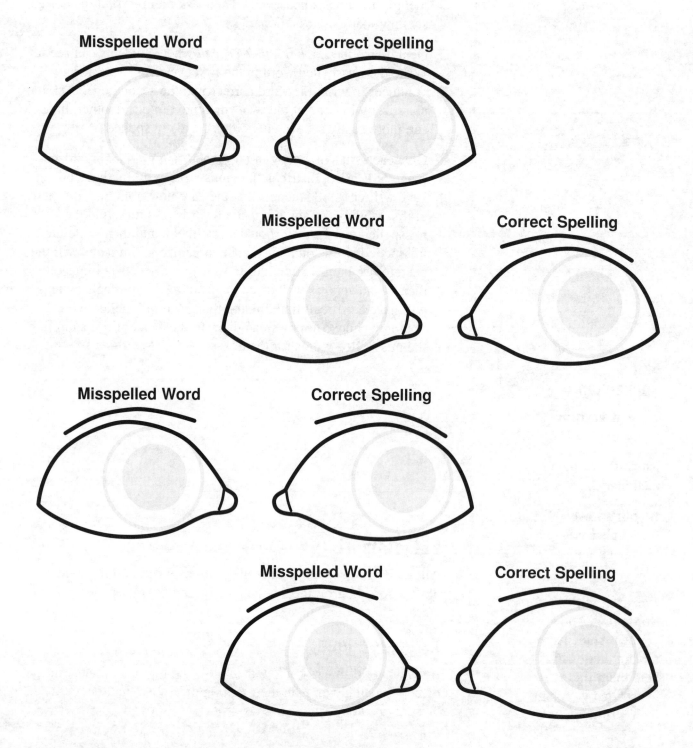

Mr. Fix It Graphic Organizer

Why Use the Graphic Organizer

- The *Mr. Fix It* graphic organizer gives peers an opportunity to edit their classmates' writings. It allows students to see how the sentences were improved by having the old sentences next to the new.

How to Use the Graphic Organizer

1. Write a sentence about yourself on the first tool of the *Mr. Fix It Overhead*. Then, ask the class how you might improve the sentence. Is there anyway you can change it to make it better? Write the students' suggestions on the second tool. Then, write a new sentence using the students' suggestions on the third tool.

2. Give students the *Mr. Fix It* graphic organizers (page 72). Ask students to write a simple sentence on their graphic organizers. They will then exchange their papers with another classmate.

3. Students will read their peers' sentences and write suggestions for making the sentence better. They will then give the graphic organizers back to the original owners.

4. Students will read their peers' suggestions and use them to improve their original sentences.

Skills Connection

Type of Writing—
narrative

Editing—applying ideas from peers

Bloom's Level—
Application
(See page 8 for a description.)

Working with Young Students: Rather than asking young students to find ways they can change their peers' work, give the class a specific way to make the sentences better, such as adding adjectives or changing the verbs.

ELL Support

Rather than asking ELL students to write out all of their suggestions for their peers on the graphic organizers, allow them to record their suggestions on tape recorders.

Extension Idea

Ask students to now find sentences in their own writings that they might improve upon. Have them complete graphic organizers with their own suggestions for different sentences on their drafts.

Name _____

Mr. Fix It

Directions: Write a sentence that could be improved on the hammer. Then, write suggestions for improving the sentence on the saw. Finally, improve the sentence on the screwdriver.

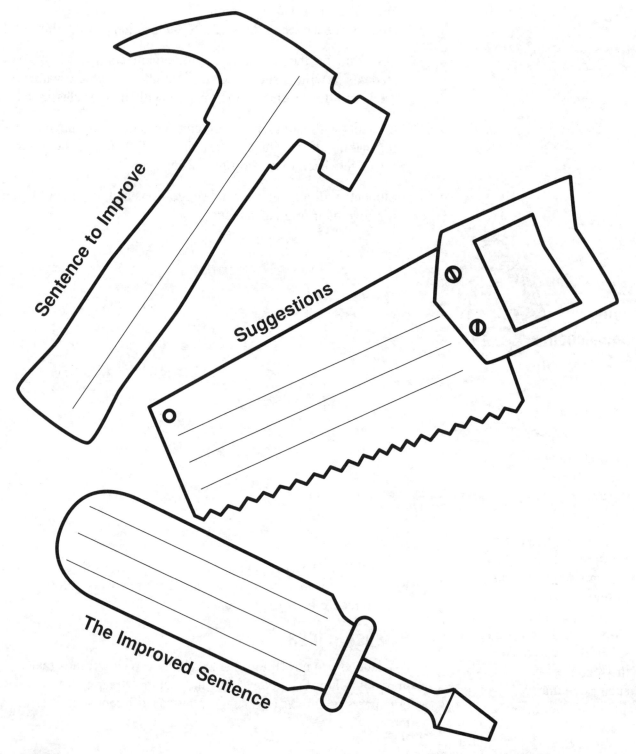

Sentence to Improve

Suggestions

The Improved Sentence

Fixing Family Memories

Standard/Objective

- **Editing:** Evaluates own and others' writing (e.g., asks questions and makes comments about writing, helps classmates apply grammatical and mechanical conventions). (McREL Language Arts, Standard 1.4)
- Students will apply their peers' suggestions in order to improve sentences in their family memories *narrative* drafts.

The Lesson

1. Ask students to close their eyes, and pretend they were pirates for Halloween. How would they be dressed? How would they look?

2. Display the *Mr. Fix It Overhead.* Then, write the following sentence on the first tool: "I put on my pirate hat and patch." Next, ask the class to think about the things they thought of as they imagined themselves as pirates. How can they make this sentence better, using the images in their minds? Write their suggestions on the second tool of the overhead. Then, use their suggestions to make the sentence better on the third tool.

3. Distribute the *Mr. Fix It* graphic organizers (page 72) to the students. Tell students that they are now going to edit their peers' *narrative* drafts. They will write one sentence that needs to be improved on the first tool and suggestions on the second tool. They will then give the graphic organizers back to the owners, along with their drafts. The owners will then improve the sentences, applying their peers' suggestions. You may choose to show students the sample graphic organizer (page 74) if they need further examples of how to create suggestions.

4. Collect the drafts so that they can be used in the *Like a Sore Thumb* revising lesson (pages 89–90).

ELL Support

Rather than asking ELL students to write out all of their suggestions for their peers' family memory *narratives* on the graphic organizers, allow them to record their suggestions on tape recorders.

Extension Idea

Ask students to now find their own sentences in their family memory *narratives* that they might improve upon. Have them complete the graphic organizers with their own suggestions, using different sentences from their drafts.

Connections to Other Lessons

Please refer to the following lessons to continue the steps in the process for creating *narrative* writing pieces.

- *Like a Sore Thumb*—pages 89–90
- *Memory Makers*—pages 121–122

Name _____

Mr. Fix It for Family Memories

Directions: Write a sentence that could be improved on the hammer. Then, write suggestions for improving the sentence on the saw. Finally, improve the sentence on the screwdriver.

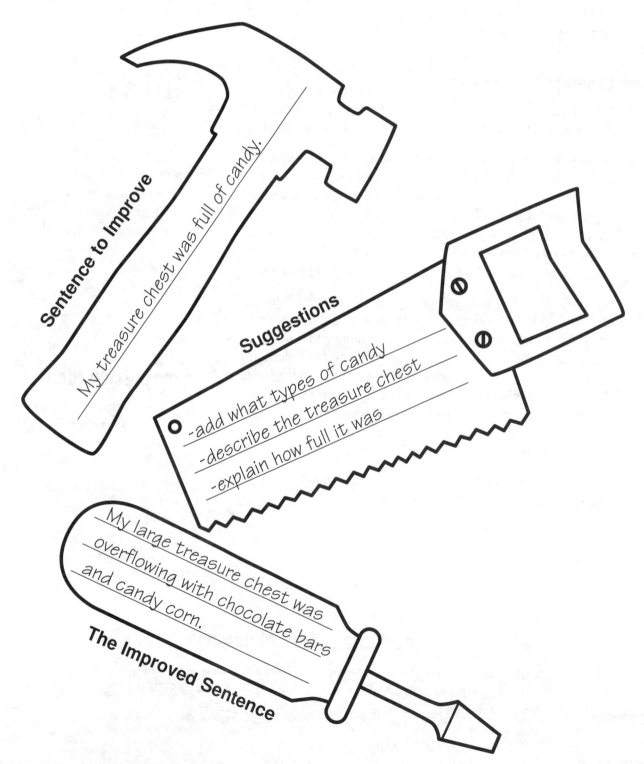

Sentence to Improve

My treasure chest was full of candy.

Suggestions

-add what types of candy
-describe the treasure chest
-explain how full it was

The Improved Sentence

My large treasure chest was overflowing with chocolate bars and candy corn.

At the End of the Rope Graphic Organizer

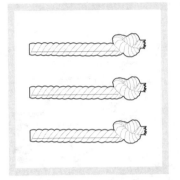

Skills Connection

Type of Writing— informational

Editing—using end punctuation

Bloom's Level—Analysis (See page 8 for a description.)

Working with Young Students: Write various statements on the *At the End of the Rope Overhead* for younger students to see, as they copy them on their own graphic organizers. Then, ask them to complete their sentences with the correct punctuation.

Why Use the Graphic Organizer

• The *At the End of the Rope* graphic organizer puts emphasis on the use of punctuation so that students can confirm the use of correct punctuation in their writing pieces.

How to Use the Graphic Organizer

1. Write several declarative sentences on the board. Then, ask the class to complete the sentences, using the correct punctuation. Review with students why and when we use periods at the end of sentences.

2. Write several more sentences on the board without punctuation. Place the *At the End of the Rope Overhead* so that students can see it. Then, ask them to look over the sentences. Allow volunteers to add the correct punctuation.

3. Give each student a copy of the *At the End of the Rope* graphic organizer (page 76). Tell the students to create three new sentences on their graphic organizers. Tell students that they also need to edit their sentences, making sure that each sentence has the correct end punctuation.

ELL Support

Give ELL students examples of both declarative sentences and questions. That way, they will have examples of when to use periods and when to use question marks. This will also help them better understand declarative sentences.

Extension Idea

Challenge students to add at least one question to their informational pieces. Have them create the questions they might add using their graphic organizers, stressing the use of question marks, rather than periods. You may also choose, as an exercise, to give students various sentences. Have them write those sentences on their graphic organizers, using the correct punctuation.

Name _____

At the End of the Rope

Directions: Write three sentences on the ropes below. Make sure you add the correct punctuation at the end of each sentence.

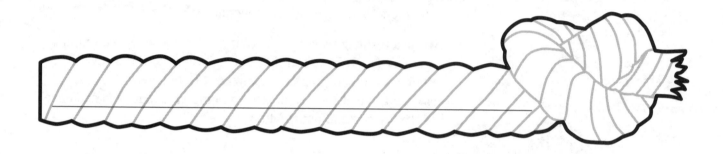

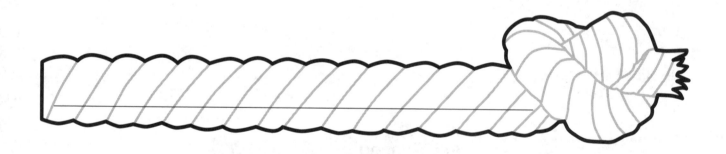

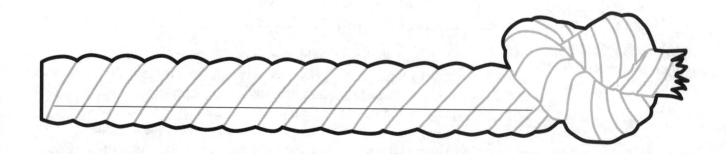

At the End of the Science Rope

Standard/Objective

- **Editing:** Uses conventions of punctuation in written compositions (e.g., uses periods after declarative sentences, uses question marks after interrogative sentences). (McREL Language Arts, Standard 3.9)
- Students will use their *At the End of the Rope* graphic organizers to create both declarative sentences and questions. They will also compare the declarative sentences to questions to ensure that correct punctuation was used.

The Lesson

1. Place students into small groups. Prior to class, draw either question marks or periods on small pieces of paper. Have each group randomly choose a piece of paper. Then, distribute the *At the End of the Rope* graphic organizers (page 76) to the students. Explain to the class that they will be creating either questions or declarative sentences in their small groups, depending on which punctuation was drawn on the pieces of paper they chose. Review the rules for using question marks and periods. Have students write their sentences on their graphic organizers. Stress that their sentences should be about the science topics they wrote about in their drafts. You may also share the sample graphic organizer (page 78) with students for yet another example.

2. Next, have the groups share their sentences with the class. Tell the class that most often, only declarative sentences are used in *informational* writing pieces, because they are stating facts in order to inform others, rather than asking questions. Distribute students' science *informational* drafts.

3. Ask students to edit their drafts, making sure that they used the correct end punctuation. You may choose to have students highlight the end punctuation on their drafts to ensure that punctuation was indeed used. Once students have edited their science drafts, collect them so that they can be used in the *One More Time* (pages 101–102) revision lesson.

ELL Support

Give ELL students examples of both declarative sentences and questions, preferably using science topics. That way, they will have examples of when to use periods and when to use question marks.

Extension Idea

Challenge students to add at least one question to their science *informational* drafts. Have them create the questions they might add using their graphic organizers, stressing the use of question marks, rather than periods. You may also choose, as an exercise, to give students various types of sentences. Have them write those sentences on their graphic organizers, using the correct punctuation. The sentences could all concern science in some way.

Connections to Other Lessons

Please refer to the following lessons to continue the steps in the process for creating *informational* writing pieces.

- *One More Time*—pages 101–102
- *Picture This*—pages 133–134

Name _____

At the End of the Rope for Seasonal Statements

Directions: Write three sentences on the ropes below. Make sure you add the correct punctuation at the end of each sentence.

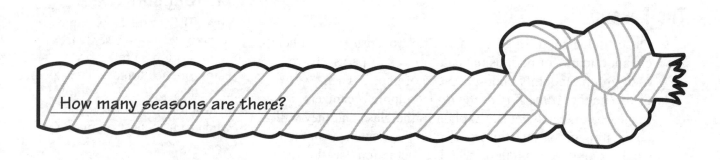

How many seasons are there?

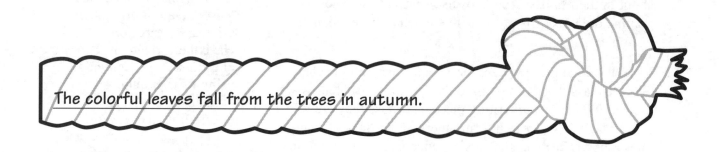

The colorful leaves fall from the trees in autumn.

Summer means hot weather and swimming pools.

Puzzle Pieces Graphic Organizer

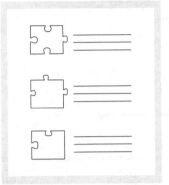

Skills Connection

Type of Writing—picture books

Editing—using complete sentences

Bloom's Level—Synthesis (See page 8 for a description.)

Working with Young Students: Help younger students understand the concept of complete sentences by providing examples of incomplete sentences. Write the examples on the board, and then allow students to complete the sentences. You may also just have younger students complete the action, or predicate portion of the sentences, rather than expecting them to complete both subjects and predicates.

Why Use the Graphic Organizer

- At this stage of writing, students may not realize that some of their sentences are incomplete. The *Puzzle Pieces* graphic organizer asks students to complete sentences, so that they can visually see the two parts of a complete sentence.

How to Use the Graphic Organizer

1. Write the following phrases on the *Puzzle Pieces Overhead,* as either the subjects or predicates of the puzzle pieces: Puzzle One: The dinosaur; Puzzle Two: fell at the park; Puzzle Three: The circus.

2. Explain to students that the above sentences are not complete. They either have no person, place, or thing doing the action, or they have no action. Ask the students to help you complete the sentences.

3. Then, distribute the *Puzzle Pieces* graphic organizers (page 80) to the students. Write three more subjects or predicates on the overhead. Have the students copy them onto their own graphic organizers. Then, ask them to complete the sentences by adding people places, or things (subjects) or actions (predicates). Review the students' answers as a class.

4. Give each student a piece of writing he or she has previously written. Ask them to edit their drafts, looking for incomplete sentences. They need to check that all of their sentences have action, and people, places, or things doing the action. Have them correct any incomplete sentences.

ELL Support

Give ELL students picture dictionaries to use as they complete their graphic organizers. This way, they can look up words that they could use to complete the sentences given to them.

Extension Idea

Encourage students to create vivid sentences by adding exciting action words and descriptive words as they edit their drafts, looking for incomplete sentences.

Name _____

Puzzle Pieces

Directions: Write the people, places, or things on the puzzle pieces. These are the subjects of your sentences. Write the action words (or verbs) on the lines.

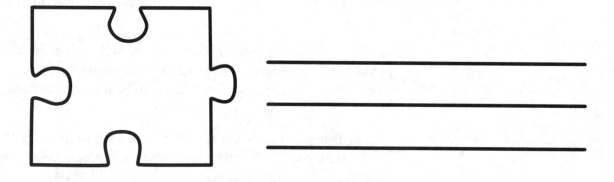

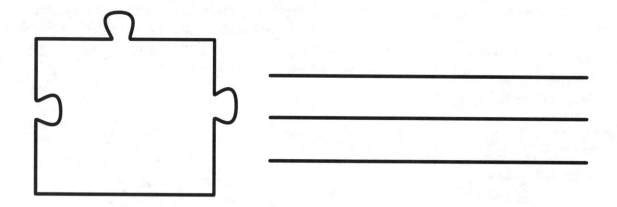

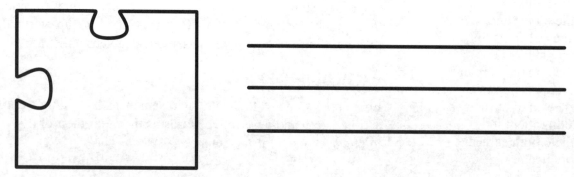

Family Puzzle Pieces

Standard/Objective

- **Editing:** Uses complete sentences in written compositions. (McREL Language Arts, Standard 3.2)
- Students will create original, complete sentences that describe their families using their *Puzzle Pieces* graphic organizers. They will then edit their family *picture books*, making sure that all of the sentences are complete.

The Lesson

1. Read the following paragraph, which has incomplete sentences, to the students: "My family. My sister. Swam at the beach. Built a sand castle. Baby brother. Went home." Ask the class what the paragraph was about. Was it easy to understand? Were there things missing in the sentences?

2. Display the *Puzzle Pieces Overhead.* Write some of the incomplete sentences from the paragraph above on the overhead. Then, ask the class to complete the sentences by adding people, places, or things to the beginning of the sentences, or action words to the end.

3. Distribute the *Puzzle Pieces* graphic organizers (page 80) to the students. Then, give them three more subjects or predicates to copy onto their graphic organizers. The subjects and predicates should be about families to go along with the theme of their *picture books.* Then, ask the students to add either subjects or predicates to the sentences to make them complete. If students need more examples of complete sentences, show them the sample graphic organizer (page 82).

4. Once students are comfortable with complete sentences, ask them to edit their family *picture book* drafts, making sure that they used complete sentences. Have them change any of their incomplete sentences to make them complete. Collect students' drafts once they are finished editing so that they can be used in *The Strongest Word* revision lesson (pages 93–94).

ELL Support

Give ELL students picture dictionaries to use as they complete their graphic organizers. This way, they can look up words that they could use to complete the example sentences about families that have been given to them.

Extension Idea

Encourage students to create vivid sentences about their families by adding exciting action words and descriptive words as they edit their drafts, looking for incomplete sentences.

Connections to Other Lessons

Please refer to the following lessons to continue the steps in the process for creating *picture books.*

- *The Strongest Word*—pages 93–94
- *Tell Me a Story*—pages 125–126

Name _____

Puzzle Pieces for Family Picture Books

Directions: Write the people, places, or things on the puzzle pieces. These are the subjects of your sentences. Write the action words (or verbs) on the lines.

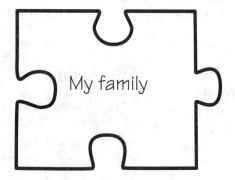

has a large space in the backyard.

_____

_____

wants to build a swing set there.

_____

_____

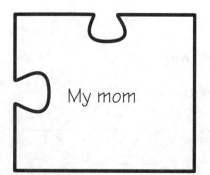

wants to plant a garden.

_____

_____

At the Car Wash Graphic Organizer

Skills Connection

Type of Writing— poetry

Editing—improving titles

Bloom's Level— Evaluation (See page 8 for a description.)

Working with Young Students: Do several examples as a class with younger students. This way, they can get more practice with making titles vivid and eye-catching before writing their own poetry titles.

Why Use the Graphic Organizer

- Students often neglect to use titles in their written works. The *At the Car Wash* graphic organizer ensures that students create titles. It also allows students to visually see titles they first develop, and then how they can improve upon those titles to make them more vivid and eye-catching.

How to Use the Graphic Organizer

1. Read various titles from books that the students read in class. Then, ask the class which titles they like the best. Why do they like them so well? Do the titles make them want to read the books?

2. Display the *At the Car Wash Overhead*. Write a title for a poem on the overhead. Then, ask the students if they feel the title is descriptive and eye-catching. What could you change to make the title even better? Change the title in some way in the second car on the overhead. Tell the students that you are "cleaning up" the title to make it more interesting. You may also choose to discuss the capitalization of titles, and which words should be capitalized, if you feel your students are able to do this.

3. Give each student a copy of the *At the Car Wash* graphic organizer (page 84). Ask the students to create titles for poems they have written or would like to write. Have them write those titles on their graphic organizers. Then, have students change at least one word to make their titles better.

ELL Support

Provide copies of poems for the ELL students. Then, allow them to view the various poetry titles, which they can use as examples when creating their own titles.

Extension Idea

Challenge students to use alliterations in their titles to make them even more exciting and catchy.

Name _____

At the Car Wash

Directions: Write the title of your poem in the first car. Then, change at least one word to make your title more vivid and interesting. Write your new title in the second car, which has gone through the car wash.

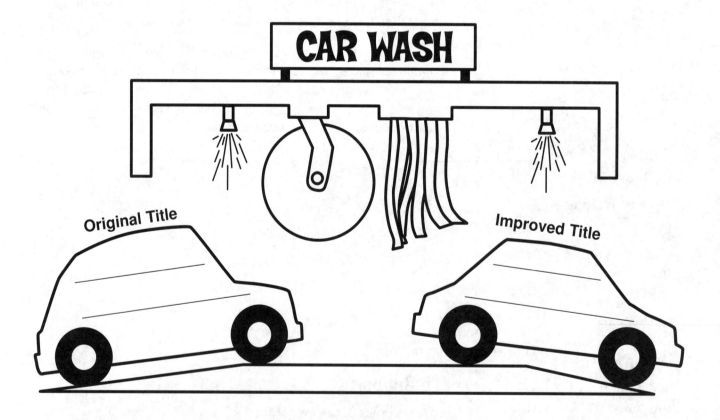

At the Animal Car Wash

Standard/Objective

- **Editing**: Uses strategies to draft and revise written work (rearranges words to improve or clarify meaning). (McREL Language Arts, Standard 1.2)
- Students will edit their *poetry* titles, changing one or two words using their *At the Car Wash* graphic organizers, in order to improve them. They will then evaluate the titles to decide which ones are best to use for their animal poems.

The Lesson

1. Read students the poem on the sample graphic organizer found in the *Poetry in Motion* lesson (page 58). Ask the students to share some good titles for the poem.

2. Display the *At the Car Wash Overhead*. Write an appropriate title for the sample poem in the first car of the overhead. Then, tell the students that you think your title is very good, but you want to make it even better. Ask them what word or words might be changed to make the title catchier. Change the title in some way to make it better. Write the new title on the second car of the overhead. Then, ask the class to vote, deciding which title they think is better. Have them give reasons for their votes. You may also choose to show students the sample graphic organizer (page 86). Then, ask them to also vote on which title they prefer, the one they created as a class, or the one found in the sample.

3. Distribute students' animal poetry drafts, as well as the *At the Car Wash* graphic organizers (page 84). Have students create titles for their animal poems on their graphic organizers. Then, have students ask themselves how they can make their titles even better. Have them improve upon their poems by changing one or two words. They should write their improved titles on their graphic organizers. Then, have the students add their titles to their drafts.

4. After students have edited their drafts, making their titles better, collect them so that they can be used in the revision lesson, *Ask Me Anything* (pages 105–106).

ELL Support

Provide copies of poems about animals for the ELL students. Then, allow them to view the various *poetry* titles, which they can use as examples when creating their own titles.

Extension Idea

Challenge students to use animal alliterations in their titles to make them even more exciting and catchy.

Connections to Other Lessons

Please refer to the following lessons to continue the steps in the process for creating *poetry*.

- *Ask Me Anything*—pages 105–106
- *Having a Ball*—pages 129–130

Name _____

At the Car Wash for Animal Poetry

Directions: Write the title of your poem in the first car. Then, change at least one word to make your title more vivid and interesting. Write your new title in the second car, which has gone through the car wash.

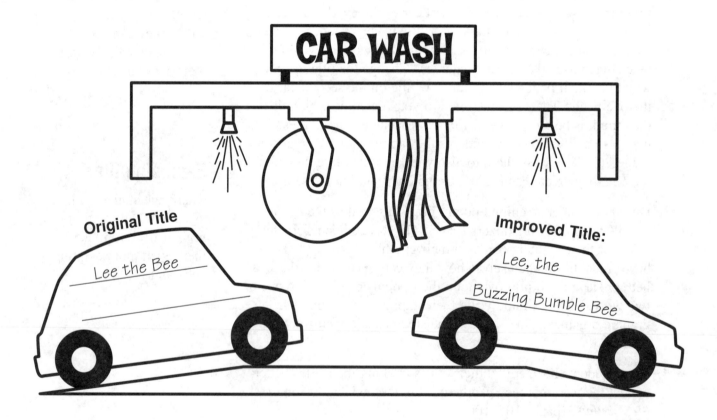

Original Title

Lee the Bee

Improved Title:

Lee, the

Buzzing Bumble Bee

Like a Sore Thumb Graphic Organizer

Skills Connection

Type of Writing— narrative

Revising—deleting extraneous information

Bloom's Level— Knowledge (See page 7 for a description.)

Working with Young Students: Give younger students several paragraphs that contain information that is not necessary or does not stay on topic. Then, allow them to delete the extra information as a class before revising their own drafts.

Why Use the Graphic Organizer

- Students often have a difficult time staying on topic. The *Like a Sore Thumb* graphic organizer asks students to write the topics from each of their sentences on their graphic organizers so that they can visually see that all sentences in their *narratives* are necessary and stay on topic. They can then use their graphic organizers as guides as they revise their drafts.

How to Use the Graphic Organizer

1. Write a paragraph about yourself on the board so that students can read it. But, make sure that there are at least two sentences that do not stay on topic or are not needed in the paragraph. Then, have students name the topics from each sentence as you write it on the fingers and palm of the *Like a Sore Thumb Overhead*. Then, ask the students if there are any topics that do not belong in your paragraph. Write the topics that do not belong on the thumb.

2. Next, show students how you should delete the sentences that do not stay on topic in your paragraph. You may also choose to have students find information that is not necessary or makes the paragraph confusing, and write that information on the sore thumb of the overhead as well.

3. Distribute the *Like a Sore Thumb* graphic organizers (page 88). Also, give students *narrative* drafts that they have previously written. Have students read their drafts and complete their graphic organizers. Then, ask them to revise their *narratives*, using their graphic organizers as guides.

ELL Support

Allow ELL students to work with partners that are higher level students. Their partners can help them determine which sentences need to be changed because they do not stay on topic.

Extension Idea

If time permits, allow students to evaluate their classmates' drafts as well, so that they can double check that all sentences stayed on topic and have only necessary information.

Name _____

Like a Sore Thumb

Directions: Read your narrative draft. Then, write the topic of each of your sentences on the hand. Are your topics all the same? Do they all belong in your paragraph? If not, write the topics that are different on the thumb. Then, revise your draft. You should delete the sentences that contain the topics on the thumb.

Revised Draft

_____

_____

_____

_____

The Sore Thumb of Family Memories

Standard/Objective

- **Revising:** Uses strategies to draft and revise written work (e.g., deletes extraneous information). (McREL Language Arts, Standard 1.2)

- Students will list the topics from each of their sentences in their family memory *narratives* using their *Like a Sore Thumb* graphic organizers. They will then check each topic to make sure that their paragraphs contain only necessary information and stay on topic.

The Lesson

1. Read the following paragraph to the students: "For Halloween this year, I dressed up like a pirate. I put on a pirate patch and a pirate hat. I like dragons too. I also found my sword and treasure chest. I found my doctor's kit. I was ready to go trick-or-treating."

2. Display the *Like a Sore Thumb Overhead*. Then, ask students what each sentence in the paragraph was about. Write the topics on the overhead. Ask them if any of the sentences were about something other than Halloween and pirates. Write any topics that didn't belong in the paragraph on the thumb. Tell students that you are now going to revise the paragraph, deleting the information that is not necessary. You may choose to model how to do this by writing the paragraph on the board or overhead, as well as by showing students the sample graphic organizer (page 90).

3. Tell students that they are now going to revise their own family memory *narratives* to make sure that they have stayed on topic, and that they don't have any extra information. Distribute their family memory *narrative* rough drafts. Also, give each student a copy of the *Like a Sore Thumb* graphic organizer (page 88). Have students complete their graphic organizers to make sure that they have only necessary information in their *narratives*.

4. Once the graphic organizers are completed, ask students to revise their drafts, deleting the sentences that did not stay on topic or that were not needed. Collect their graphic organizers to be used in the publishing lesson, *Memory Makers,* found on pages 121–122.

ELL Support

Allow ELL students to work with partners that are higher-level students. Their partners can help them determine which sentences need to be changed in their family memory *narratives*.

Extension Idea

If time permits, allow students to evaluate their classmates' family *narrative* drafts as well, so that they can double check that all sentences stayed on topic and have only necessary information.

Connections to Other Lessons

Please refer to the following lessons to continue the steps in the process for creating *narrative* writing pieces.

- *Memory Makers*—pages 121–122

Name _____

Like a Sore Thumb for Family Memory Narratives

Directions: Read your narrative draft. Then, write the topic of each of your sentences on the hand. Are your topics all the same? Do they all belong in your paragraph? If not, write the topics that are different on the thumb. Then, revise your draft. You should delete the sentences that contain the topics on the thumb.

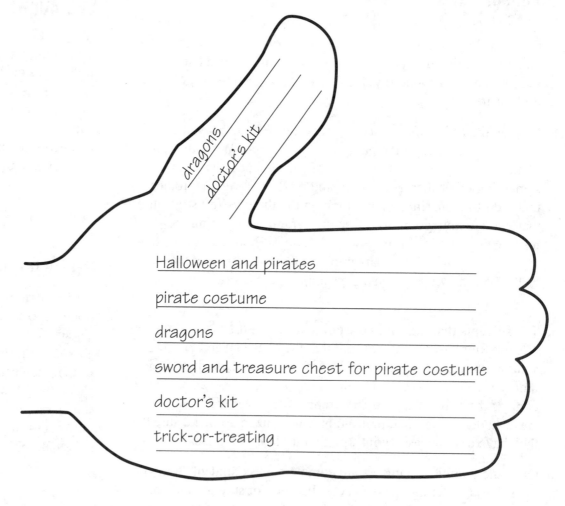

dragons

doctor's kit

Halloween and pirates

pirate costume

dragons

sword and treasure chest for pirate costume

doctor's kit

trick-or-treating

Revised Draft

For Halloween this year, I dressed up like a pirate. I put on a pirate patch and a pirate hat. I also found my sword and treasure chest. I was ready to go trick-or-treating.

The Strongest Word Graphic Organizer

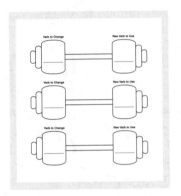

Skills Connection

Type of Writing— picture books

Revising—using verbs in writing

Bloom's Level— Comprehension (See page 7 for a description.)

Working with Young Students: Allow younger students to have action words to refer to by making a list as a class of strong verbs they could use in their writings.

Why Use the Graphic Organizer

• Strong verbs are important in making writing unique and vivid. *The Strongest Word* graphic organizer allows students to apply their knowledge of verbs in order to compare verbs they have used to stronger verbs that may be used in their *picture books*.

How to Use the Graphic Organizer

1. Review action words with students by having them "act out" several verbs. Then, tell them that verbs are important to stories. Verbs tell us what the characters are doing, and help us form pictures in our minds.

2. Give students copies of a sample paragraph from a textbook. Tell them that it is important that they use strong verbs in their writings. Have students circle all of the verbs in the sample paragraph. Then, place *The Strongest Word Overhead* so that students can see it. Ask for volunteers to read some of the verbs they circled. Write the verbs in the first part of the barbells on the overhead. Next, ask the class if they could change the verbs to make them stronger. Change the verbs to make them more vivid.

3. Distribute *The Strongest Word* graphic organizers (page 92). Have students choose three verbs from drafts that they have previously written. Have them record those verbs on their graphic organizers. Then, have students list stronger verbs to replace the other action words on their graphic organizers as well. Ask students to then revise their drafts, making the three verbs they changed stronger.

ELL Support

Give ELL students thesauruses to use as they change their drafts. This way, they can find synonyms for the verbs they wish to change.

Extension Idea

To further help students understand verbs and use them in their writings, challenge them to create dictionaries of verbs that could be used in their writings. You may also create a contest of who can create the largest verb dictionary containing the most verbs.

Name _____

The Strongest Word

Directions: Write a verb from your draft that you feel could be stronger on the left side of each barbell. Then, change the verb by writing a new one on the right side of each barbell.

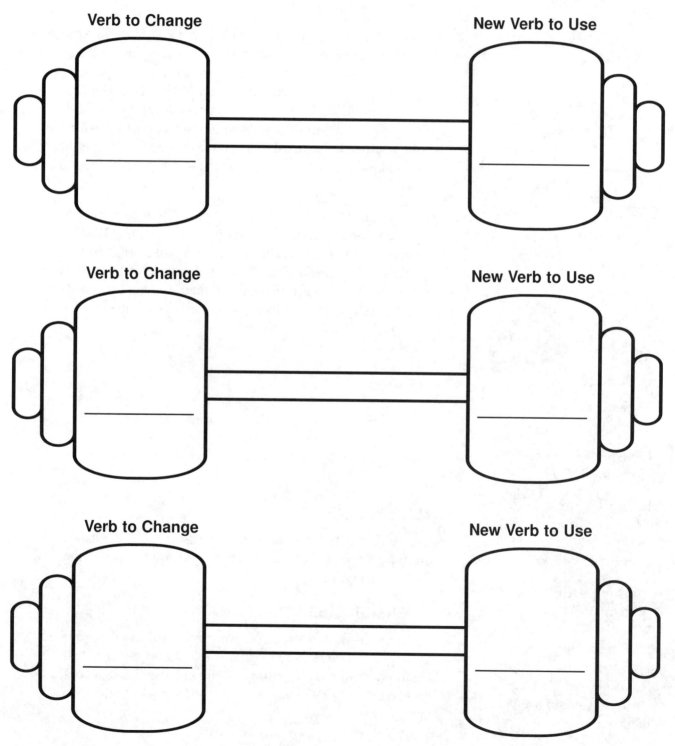

The Family's Strongest Word

Standard/Objective

- **Revising:** Uses verbs in written compositions (e.g., verbs for a variety of situations, action words). (McREL Language Arts, Standard 3.4)
- Students will use their knowledge of verbs, as well as their *The Strongest Word* graphic organizers, to write stronger verbs that could replace other verbs used in their *picture books*.

The Lesson

1. Read a *picture book* to the students. Then, write three overused verbs that were written in the *picture book* on *The Strongest Word Overhead*. Ask students if they can think of other verbs that might be used instead of the three you listed to make the *picture book* more vivid. Write their ideas on the overhead. You may show students the sample graphic organizer (page 94) as an example of verbs that can be made stronger.

2. Distribute students' family *picture book* drafts, as well as *The Strongest Word* graphic organizers (page 92). Ask students to highlight the verbs they used in their stories. Then, ask them to choose three verbs that could be stronger, or more vivid. Have them use their graphic organizers to change the verbs.

3. Once students have completed their organizers, have them revise their picture books, using the stronger verbs. Collect students' drafts once they are revised, so that they can be used in the *Tell Me a Story* publishing lesson (pages 125–126).

ELL Support

Give ELL students thesauruses to use as they change their family *picture book* drafts. This way, they can find synonyms for the verbs they wish to change.

Extension Idea

To further help students understand verbs and use them in their writings, challenge them to create dictionaries of verbs that could be used in their family *picture books*. You may also create a contest of who can create the largest verb dictionary containing the most verbs.

Connections to Other Lessons

Please refer to the following lessons to continue the steps in the process for creating *picture books*.

- *Tell Me a Story*—pages 125–126

Name _____

The Strongest Word for Family Stories

Directions: Write a verb from your draft that you feel could be stronger on the left side of each barbell. Then, change the verb by writing a new one on the right side of each barbell.

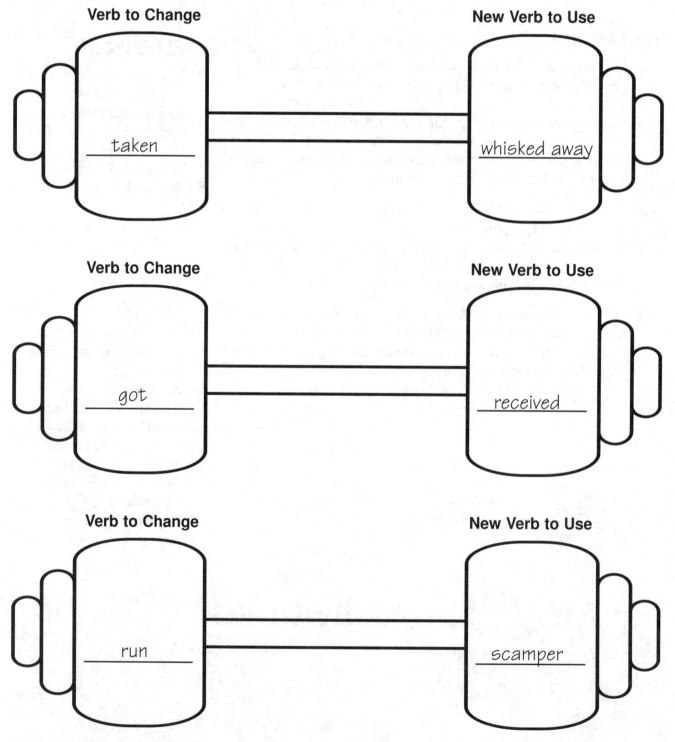

Verb to Change　　　　　　　　　　　**New Verb to Use**

taken　　　　　　　　　　　whisked away

Verb to Change　　　　　　　　　　　**New Verb to Use**

got　　　　　　　　　　　received

Verb to Change　　　　　　　　　　　**New Verb to Use**

run　　　　　　　　　　　scamper

Vegetable Variety Graphic Organizer

Skills Connection

Type of Writing— friendly letter

Revising—varying sentence type

Bloom's Level— Application (See page 8 for a description.)

Working with Young Students: Divide the lesson into two to three days for younger students. This way, they can concentrate on statements one day and questions the next, rather than having to learn both types of sentences in one day.

Why Use the Graphic Organizer

- Students often use the same sentence types in their writings. The *Vegetable Variety* graphic organizer forces students to examine the types of sentences used in their writings, guaranteeing sentence variety.

How to Use the Graphic Organizer

1. Write a paragraph on the board that is composed of only questions. Ask the class if the paragraph is well written. What might need to be changed to make the paragraph better? Explain to the class that when writing letters or other forms of writing, it is important to create a variety of sentence types, in order to make the writing interesting. Review statements and questions with students, as well as what type of punctuation is necessary for each. Then, ask them how you might change your paragraph to make it better by varying the sentence type.

2. Next, place the *Vegetable Variety Overhead* so that students can see it. Ask them to now count the number of statements in your improved paragraph. Record the amount on the overhead. Do the same for questions. Explain to students that you do not have to have exactly the same amount of the two types of sentences, but you shouldn't have a lot more of one over the other. Then, have the students create two new sentences that you could add to the paragraph in order to have more variety.

3. Next, distribute the *Vegetable Variety* graphic organizers (page 96). Have each student compose a *friendly letter* to a classmate. Then, ask the class to revise their drafts by completing their graphic organizers, then adding sentence variety to their letters.

ELL Support

Provide ELL students with lists of example questions and statements, which they can refer to as they revise their *friendly letters*.

Extension Idea

Encourage students to also use exclamatory sentences in their *friendly letters*.

Name _____

Vegetable Variety

Directions: Count the number of statements used in your writing. Write the number on the tomato. Then, count the number of questions used. Write that number on the carrot. Do you have more questions or statements? Create two new sentences that you could add in order to vary the sentence type. Write those sentences on the corn.

Number of Statements

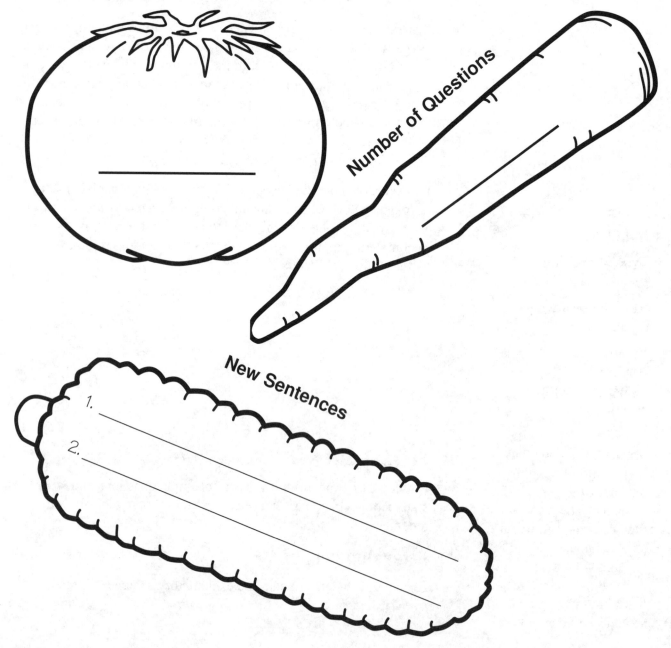

Number of Questions

New Sentences

1. _____
2. _____

A Variety of Pen Pal Letters

Standard/Objective

- **Revising:** Uses strategies to draft and revise written work (e.g., varies sentence type). (McREL Language Arts, Standard 1.2)
- Students will apply their knowledge of statements and questions as they check for sentence variety when revising their pen pal letters, using the *Vegetable Variety* graphic organizers. They will then create new sentences to add to their drafts that will ensure sentence variety.

The Lesson

1. Write three statements and three questions that might be included in *friendly letters* on the board. Ask students to identify which of the sentences are statements and which are questions. Explain to the class that it is important to use sentence variety when writing *friendly letters*. They should tell the recipients of their letters interesting news and facts, but they should ask questions in their letters as well. Also explain to students that even if they have the same number of statements and questions in their paragraphs, they should not list all of the statements in a row, then all of the questions. It is important that they vary the order of their sentences within their letters to make their paragraphs flow.

2. Display the *Vegetable Variety Overhead*. Then, read the friendly letter found in the *Building a Letter* sample graphic organizer (page 62). Ask students to identify the number of statements and questions found in the letter. Record them on the overhead. Then, show students the *Vegetable Variety* sample graphic organizer (page 98) for examples of other sentences that might be added to allow for a greater amount of sentence variety in the *friendly letter*.

3. Distribute the *Vegetable Variety* graphic organizers (page 96) to the students. Also distribute students' *friendly letter* drafts. Explain to the class that they are now going to revise their drafts to make sure that they have sentence variety. Have them complete their graphic organizers and then change their drafts, adding the necessary sentence types to allow for a variety of sentences. Once students have revised their drafts, collect them so that they can be used in the *In the Mail* publishing lesson, (pages 117–118).

ELL Support

Provide ELL students with lists of example questions and statements that they might use in their drafts as they revise their pen pal *friendly letters*.

Extension Idea

Encourage students to also use exclamatory sentences in their pen pal *friendly letters*.

Connections to Other Lessons

Please refer to the following lessons to continue the steps in the process for creating *friendly letters*.

- *In the Mail*—pages 117–118

Name _____

Vegetable Variety for Pen Pal Letters

Directions: Count the number of statements used in your writing. Write the number on the tomato. Then, count the number of questions used. Write that number on the carrot. Do you have more questions or statements? Create two new sentences that you could add in order to vary the sentence type. Write those sentences on the corn.

Number of Statements

4

Number of Questions

2

New Sentences

1. Do you have any hobbies?

2. How would you describe yourself?

One More Time Graphic Organizer

Skills Connection

Type of Writing— informational

Revising—rereading the text

Bloom's Level— Analysis (See page 8 for a description.)

Working with Young Students: Allow younger students to reread their *informational* drafts aloud with partners. This way, their partners can help them find the mistakes that they may not find on their own.

Why Use the Graphic Organizer

- The *One More Time* graphic organizer allows students to compare the errors they find in their first readings of their drafts to those mistakes they find by rereading their works a second time. This graphic organizer shows students the importance of revising texts by reading them more than once, as they will visually see the errors that they found after their second readings.

How to Use the Graphic Organizer

1. Place an *informational* paragraph on the board so that students can see it. Make sure that the paragraph has several mistakes in it. Read the paragraph to the class. Tell the class that there are several mistakes in the paragraph. Ask one volunteer to tell you what mistakes he/she sees. Write the mistakes on the first clock of the *One More Time Overhead*.

2. Then, tell students to read the paragraph once again. Ask the class if they found more mistakes that they had not found in their first reading of the paragraph. Write the mistakes they found by reading the paragraph a second time in the second clock on the overhead.

3. Tell students it is very important to read their drafts more than once so that they can find all of the revisions that need to be made. Distribute the *One More Time* graphic organizers (page 100) to the students. Have students take out *informational* drafts that they have previously written. Have the students read their drafts once, noting any mistakes on their organizers. Then, have them read their drafts once again, noting the mistakes they found the second time as well. After they have found their mistakes, ask them to revise their drafts, fixing any errors that they might have found.

ELL Support

ELL students might benefit by having their drafts read aloud to them, so that they can find the errors that they hear, as well as see.

Extension Idea

Encourage students to read their drafts three to four times to look for even more errors.

Name _____

One More Time

Directions: Read your draft once. Then, write the things that need to be revised in the first clock. Read your draft a second time. Write the errors you found after the second reading in the second clock.

First Reading

1. _____
   _____
   _____
2. _____
   _____
   _____
3. _____
   _____
   _____

Second Reading

1. _____
   _____
2. _____
   _____
3. _____
   _____

Reading About Science
One More Time

Standard/Objective

- **Revising:** Uses strategies to draft and revise written work (e.g., rereads). (McREL Language Arts, Standard 1.2)
- Students will revise their science *informational* drafts by finding revisions that need to be made when reading their drafts at least two times. They will write those revisions on their *One More Time* graphic organizers, as well as correcting their drafts.

The Lesson

1. Write the four seasons paragraph found in the sample lesson (page 102) onto the bottom of the *One More Time Overhead*. The paragraph contains simple errors that students can find. Then, allow students to view the paragraph as you read it aloud to them. Ask a volunteer to find the errors in the paragraph. List the errors the volunteer found on the first clock. Then, have the class read the paragraph again. Have another volunteer list the errors he/she found the second time by rereading the paragraph. Write those errors in the second clock. You may also compare the sample graphic organizer (page 102) to the mistakes the students listed to make sure all errors were found.

2. Tell students that it is important to read their drafts more than once so that they can make all of the necessary revisions. Also explain to them that revisions can be errors found in their writings, as well as ways to improve their writing by changing words or adding information. Distribute students' science informational drafts, as well as the *One More Time* graphic organizers (page 100). Ask them to read their drafts and list the errors they find in their first readings on their graphic organizers. Then, have students read their drafts a second time, finding more revisions that need to be made.

3. Once students have found the necessary revisions, ask them to improve their drafts by making the corrections listed on their graphic organizers. Then, collect their drafts to be used in the publishing lesson, *Picture This,* (pages 133–134).

ELL Support

ELL students might benefit by having their science *informational* drafts read aloud to them, so that they can find the errors that they hear, as well as see.

Extension Idea

Encourage students to read their science *informational* drafts three to four times to look for even more revisions that can be made.

Connections to Other Lessons

Please refer to the following lessons to continue the steps in the process for creating *informational* writing pieces.

- *Picture This*—pages 133–134

Name _____

One More Time for Science Informational Drafts

Directions: Read your draft once. Then, write the things that need to be revised in the first clock. Read your draft a second time. Write the errors you found after the second reading in the second clock.

First Reading

1. The second sentence is not complete.

2. "Leaves" is spelled wrong in the third sentence.

3. Weather is spelled wrong in the fifth sentence.

Second Reading

1. Change the word "winter" in the last sentence to make the sentence sound better.

2. There needs to be a comma after spring in the first sentence.

3. It should be "too," not "two" in "Fall is called autumn, too."

Ask Me Anything Graphic Organizer

Skills Connection

Type of Writing— poetry

Revising—asking questions about writing

Bloom's Level— Synthesis (See page 8 for a description.)

Working with Young Students: Rather than having younger students create questions on their own, using their graphic organizers, create questions about their writings as a class, then have students record one of those questions to answer on their graphic organizers.

Why Use the Graphic Organizer

- The *Ask Me Anything* graphic organizer gives students the opportunity to reexamine their drafts. With questions written for them to answer concerning their writings, as well as an opportunity to develop their own questions, students can see the things that might need to be revised in their poems by using their graphic organizers.

How to Use the Graphic Organizer

1. Read a poem to the students. It can be one from a book or one you have written. Then, place the *Ask Me Anything Overhead* where students can see it. Review the questions with the class that are written on the overhead. Then, have students answer the questions concerning the poem that was read aloud. Once students have answered the questions, ask them to think of other good questions to ask about the poem. Write an original question on the space provided, along with an answer to it.

2. Tell students that it is important to ask questions about their writings to make sure that nothing needs to be changed or improved. Distribute the *Ask Me Anything* graphic organizers (page 104). Have students take out poetry drafts that they have written, or have students draft short poems. Tell them to reread their drafts, answering the questions on their graphic organizers. Then, have the students create their own questions that they could ask concerning their poems. Have them also answer their original questions. Finally, ask students to revise their poems, using the answers from their graphic organizers.

ELL Support

Allow ELL students to answer their questions using phrases rather than complete sentences. This will allow them to focus on the answers, rather than worrying about writing their answers in complete sentences.

Extension Idea

Challenge students to create more than one question to ask about their writings on their graphic organizers.

Name _____

Ask Me Anything

Directions: After reading your poetry draft, answer the questions below. Then, write a question that would be helpful for improving your draft on the lines. Be sure you also answer that question.

Does My Poem Rhyme?

Does My Poem Make Sense?

Ask the Animals Anything

Standard/Objective

- **Revising:** Evaluates own and others' writing (e.g., asks questions about writing). (McREL Language Arts, Standard 1.4)

- Students will answer questions about their writings in order to improve their poems using their *Ask Me Anything* graphic organizers. They will then create their own questions about their poems that can be used as an evaluation tool.

The Lesson

1. Show students the bee poem, found in the *Poetry in Motion* sample graphic organizer (page 58). Then, display the *Ask Me Anything Overhead.* Ask students to answer the questions concerning the poem. Then, ask them how they could improve the poem using the answers to the questions. Finally, ask them what other questions they could create to evaluate the poem. Questions students might create are "Does the poem stay on topic?" or "Can the poem be changed to make it more interesting?" You may also show students the sample graphic organizer (page 106) to compare their answers to those on the sample.

2. Once students understand how answering the questions can help them realize how their poems should be revised, distribute their animal poems. Also, give each student a copy of the *Ask Me Anything* graphic organizer (page 104). Have students read their own animal poems. Then, ask them to complete their graphic organizers by answering the questions, along with creating their own questions to answer, concerning their animal poems.

3. Once students have evaluated their poems by answering the questions, ask them to revise their poems, using their answers on their graphic organizers as guides. After students' revisions are complete, collect their drafts to be used in the publishing lesson, *Having a Ball* (pages 129–130).

ELL Support

Allow ELL students to answer their questions using phrases rather than complete sentences when evaluating their animal poems. This will allow them to focus on the answers, rather than worrying about writing their answers in complete sentences.

Extension Idea

Challenge students to create more than one question to ask about their animal poems on their graphic organizers.

Connections to Other Lessons

Please refer to the following lessons to continue the steps in the process for creating *poetry*.

- *Having a Ball*—pages 129–130

Name _____

Ask Me Anything for Animal Poems

Directions: After reading your poetry draft, answer the questions below. Then, write a question that would be helpful for improving your draft on the lines. Be sure you also answer that question.

Does My Poem Rhyme?

My poem does
rhyme. All of my last
words end in the "ee" sound.

Does My Poem Make Sense?

My poem is a little
silly, but it makes sense.
My sentences explain the
bee in the tree and what he
does.

What else can I add to my poem? I can change my poem by
adding more lines or maybe more characters. The bee could
meet someone while in the tree, such as maybe a flea.

Lending a Hand Graphic Organizer

Why Use the Graphic Organizer

- The *Lending a Hand* graphic organizer allows students to organize their thoughts and suggestions as they improve upon their own and their peers' *descriptive* writings.

How to Use the Graphic Organizer

1. Write the following sentence in the palm of the *Lending a Hand Overhead*: "The dog ran down the street." Then, place the class into small groups. Ask each group to make one suggestion for making the sentence more descriptive or vivid. Write the groups' suggestions on the fingers of the overhead. Then, improve the sentence using at least one of the suggestions on the lines at the bottom of the graphic organizer.

2. Explain to the class that they are now going to edit their peers' *descriptive* writing pieces. Have the class stay in the same small groups. Distribute the *Lending a Hand* graphic organizers (page 108), as well as *descriptive* rough drafts that students have written. Have students choose a sentence they feel could be improved from their drafts. Have them write that sentence on the palm of their graphic organizers. Then, have each student trade papers with each group member, so that all group members can make one suggestion for improving the sentence on each of their peer's graphic organizers.

3. Once all group members have made suggestions, have students read the suggestions on their graphic organizers, and then improve their sentences. They should write their improved sentences on the bottom of their graphic organizers. Tell students to also change their sentences on their drafts as well.

Skills Connection

Type of Writing— descriptive

Revising—incorporates peers' suggestions

Bloom's Level— Evaluation (See page 8 for a description.)

Working with Young Students: Do several examples of how to improve sentences with younger students. This way, they are more confident when they edit others' work.

ELL Support

Place ELL students in small groups with higher-level students. This way, they can have help with writing their suggestions on the graphic organizers.

Extension Idea

Encourage students to use thesauruses to change the verbs of the sentences in order to make them more vivid, rather than just adding adjectives.

Name _____

Lending a Hand

Directions: Write a sentence you would like to improve on the palm of the hand below. Then, ask your classmates to make four suggestions for improving the sentence on the fingers. Finally, write a new, improved sentence on the lines below the hand.

_____

_____

_____

_____

Lending a Hand for Toys

Standard/Objective

- **Revising:** Uses strategies to draft and revise written work (e.g., incorporates suggestions from peers and teachers). (McREL Language Arts, Standard 1.2)
- Students will evaluate their peers' writings in order to offer suggestions for improving sentences. They will then write those suggestions on the *Lending a Hand* graphic organizers.

The Lesson

1. Bring a stuffed clown to class. Ask the students to describe the clown. Write one of the sentences the students give on the *Lending a Hand Overhead*.

2. Tell students that the sentence is great, but it can be even better. Ask them for suggestions to improve the sentence. Write their suggestions on the fingers of the overhead. Then, change the sentence, making it better, on the lines below the hand. Show students the sample graphic organizer (page 110) for another example of suggestions for improving a sentence.

3. Tell students that they are now going to help their classmates improve their writings by offering suggestions. Distribute students' toy *descriptive* drafts, as well as the *Lending a Hand* graphic organizers (page 108). Tell students that they are now going to choose one sentence from their drafts that they wish to improve. They should then ask five classmates to write suggestions on their graphic organizers for improving their sentences. Once the suggestions have been made, students will decide how they should change the sentence, and do so on their graphic organizers, as well as on their drafts. Remind students that they don't have to use all of their peers' suggestions.

4. Once students have revised their drafts, collect them for later use in the publishing lesson, *Share the Love* (pages 113–114).

ELL Support

Place ELL students in small groups with higher level students. This way, they will have help when writing their suggestions for improving the toy descriptions on the graphic organizers.

Extension Idea

Encourage students to use thesauruses to change the verbs of the toy descriptions in order to make them more vivid, rather than just adding adjectives.

Connections to Other Lessons

Please refer to the following lessons to continue the steps in the process for creating *descriptive* writing pieces.

- *Share the Love*—pages 113–114

Name _____

Lending a Hand for Describing a Toy

Directions: Write a sentence you would like to improve on the palm of the hand below. Then, ask your classmates to make suggestions for improving the sentence on the fingers. Finally, write a new, improved sentence on the lines below the hand.

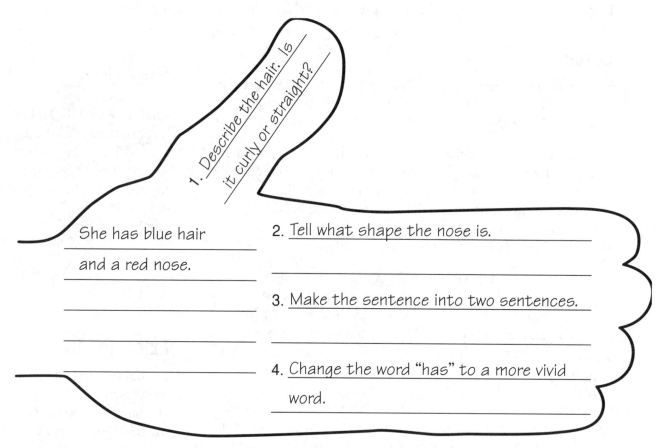

1. Describe the hair. Is it curly or straight?

She has blue hair and a red nose.

2. Tell what shape the nose is.

3. Make the sentence into two sentences.

4. Change the word "has" to a more vivid word.

My clown has springy blue hair that bounces back when you pull it.

Her round, red nose can be seen from miles away!

_____

Share the Love Graphic Organizer

Skills Connection

Type of Writing— descriptive

Publishing—sharing the finished product

Bloom's Level— Knowledge (See page 7 for a description.)

Working with Young Students: Rather than having younger students individually brainstorm ways to share their final copies, complete the graphic organizers as a class.

Why Use the Graphic Organizer

• Brainstorming is an important skill for students, as it helps them develop the best plan for their writings. The *Share the Love* graphic organizer allows students to brainstorm various ways to share their final writing products with their classmates, while encouraging creativity.

How to Use the Graphic Organizer

1. Give students revised *descriptive* drafts that they have written. Then, ask them to create final copies, making sure that all revisions have been made.

2. Once students have completed their final copies, place the *Share the Love Overhead* where students can see it. Tell students that you now want them to think of creative ways they can share their final copies with the class. Write some ways on the overhead. You may wish to refer to the sample graphic organizer (page 114) for ideas.

3. Give each student a copy of the *Share the Love* graphic organizer (page 112). Then, ask them to think of their own ways that they would like to share their final copies. Once students have brainstormed lists of ways to share their descriptions on their graphic organizers, have each student choose one way to share his or her final copy with the class.

4. Allow students to prepare their presentations, and then share their final copies with the class.

ELL Support

Allow ELL students to draw pictures of their ideas, rather than writing them.

Extension Idea

If time is limited, you may have students share their final copies in small groups, using their presentation ideas, rather than sharing with the entire class.

Name _____

Share the Love

Directions: Brainstorm a list of ways you can share your writing with the class. Write those ways in the hearts below.

Share the Love of Toys

Standard/Objective

- **Publishing:** Uses strategies to edit and publish written work (e.g., shares finished product). (McREL Language Arts, Standard 1.3)
- Students will brainstorm lists of ways to share their toy descriptions using their *Share the Love* graphic organizers. They will then use their final copies to prepare their presentations that will be shared with the class.

The Lesson

1. Give students their toy *descriptive* rough drafts. Ask them to write their final copies for their toy descriptions, making sure they have made all revisions.

2. Then, read the following paragraph to the students: "My favorite toy is Funny the ____. She has blue hair and a red nose. My toy wears silly glasses and a shirt with dots. Funny has large feet and curly hair." Then, ask the class what they think the toy is. Tell them that it is more fun to present writings to the class if they do it in creative ways, such as through guessing games, picture books, or advertisements.

3. Distribute the *Share the Love* graphic organizers (page 112) to the students. Then, ask the students to use their organizers to brainstorm various ways they could share their final copies with the class, without just simply reading them aloud. Allow students to refer to the sample graphic organizer (page 114) if they are struggling with ideas.

4. Once students have completed their graphic organizers, and have decided on the ways they wish to present their toy descriptions to the class, allow them to prepare their presentations. Then, have the students share their final copies with their classmates.

ELL Support

Allow ELL students to draw pictures of their ideas for sharing their toy descriptions, rather than writing them.

Extension Idea

If time is limited, you may have students share their toy descriptions in small groups, using their presentation ideas, rather than sharing with the entire class.

Connections to Other Lessons

Please refer to the following lessons to continue the steps in the process for creating *descriptive* writing pieces.

- *Bright Ideas*—pages 25–26
- *A Shower of Words*—pages 41–42
- *Look It Up*—pages 69–70
- *Lending a Hand*—pages 109–110

Name _____

Share the Love for Toy Descriptions

Directions: Brainstorm a list of ways you can share your writing with the class. Write those ways in the hearts below.

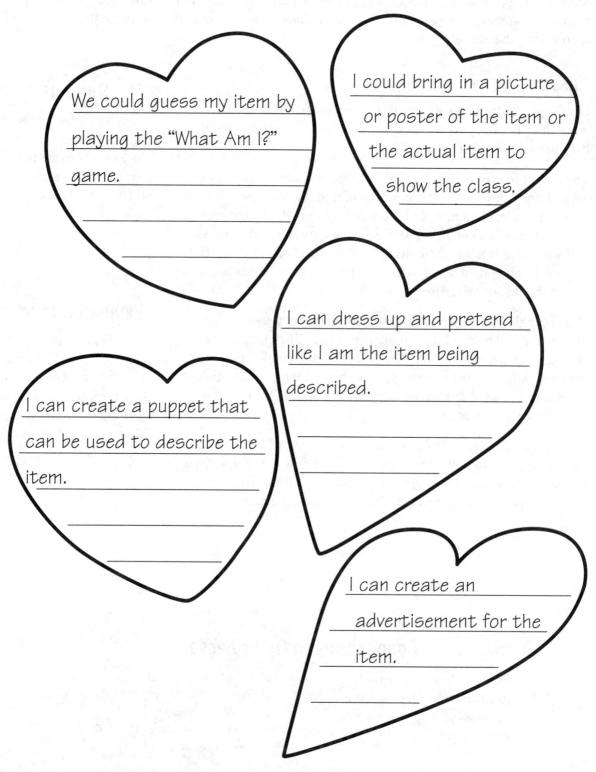

We could guess my item by playing the "What Am I?" game.

I could bring in a picture or poster of the item or the actual item to show the class.

I can dress up and pretend like I am the item being described.

I can create a puppet that can be used to describe the item.

I can create an advertisement for the item.

In the Mail Graphic Organizer

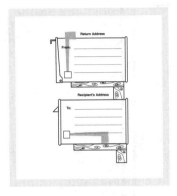

Why Use the Graphic Organizer

- Writing addresses is a necessary life skill. The *In the Mail* graphic organizer allows students to practice writing addresses before mailing their *friendly letters* to the recipients.

How to Use the Graphic Organizer

1. Have students write short letters to their friends. Students should use proper greetings, closings, and dates.

2. Display the *In the Mail Overhead*. Show students the proper way to write addresses on the overhead. You may also choose to discuss the difference between a return address and the recipient's address. Then, give each student a copy of the *In the Mail* graphic organizer (page 116). Ask students to practice writing their return addresses, as well as their recipients' addresses, on their organizers.

3. Once students have correctly written the addresses on their organizers, distribute envelopes for them to write their final copies of the addresses. Show students where to write the addresses on the envelopes. Then, allow them to mail their *friendly letters*, or ask them to take them home to mail.

Skills Connection

Type of Writing— friendly letter

Publishing—writing addresses

Bloom's Level— Comprehension (See page 7 for a description.)

Working with Young Students: Allow younger students to gain practice writing addresses by practicing the school's address as a class on large envelopes made from poster board or butcher paper.

ELL Support

Provide ELL students with atlases or other resources that contain lists of cities and states. This will help them as they complete their addresses on both their envelopes and their graphic organizers.

Extension Idea

Allow students to create original stationery using blank paper. They can include personal items or objects that the people to whom they wrote would enjoy.

Name _____

In the Mail

Directions: Practice writing the return address and the recipient's address on the mailboxes below.

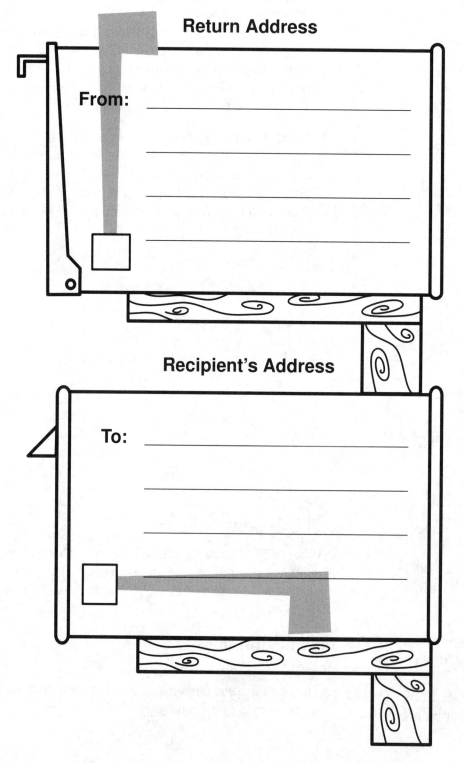

Return Address

From:

Recipient's Address

To:

It's in the Mail to My Pen Pal

Standard/Objective

- **Publishing:** Writes personal letters (e.g., addresses envelopes). (McREL Language Arts, Standard 1.12, Level II)
- Students will use their *In the Mail* graphic organizers to practice writing their own addresses as well as the addresses of their pen pals.

The Lesson

1. Give students their pen pal *friendly letter* drafts. Then, ask them to create their final copies. You may allow them to use stationery for their final copies. Be sure that students include the proper greetings and closings, as well as the date.

2. Write the addresses from the sample lesson (page 118) on the *In the Mail Overhead*. Then, show students the *In the Mail Overhead*, modeling how to write addresses. Also discuss the difference between a return address and the recipient's address.

3. Next, distribute the *In the Mail* graphic organizers (page 116) to the students. Ask them to practice writing their own addresses, as well as their pen pals' addresses, on their graphic organizers. Once students are comfortable with writing addresses, allow them to write their addresses on actual envelopes. You may choose to have students write their pen pals' names, and then the school's address, on the recipient portion of their graphic organizers.

4. Allow students to mail their letters to their pen pals, or you may choose to arrange a time when the classes involved can hand-deliver their letters.

ELL Support

Provide ELL students with atlases or other resources that contain lists of cities and states. This will help them as they complete their addresses on both their envelopes and their graphic organizers for their pen pal *friendly letters*.

Extension Idea

Allow students to create original stationery using blank paper. They can include personal items or objects that their pen pals would enjoy, or that they enjoy.

Connections to Other Lessons

Please refer to the following lessons to continue the steps in the process for creating *friendly letters*.

- *Snapshots of Me*—pages 37–38
- *Building a Letter*—pages 61–62
- *The Name Game*—pages 65–66
- *Vegetable Variety*—pages 97–98

Name _____

In the Mail for My Pen Pal Friendly Letter

Directions: Practice writing the return address and the recipient's address on the mailboxes below.

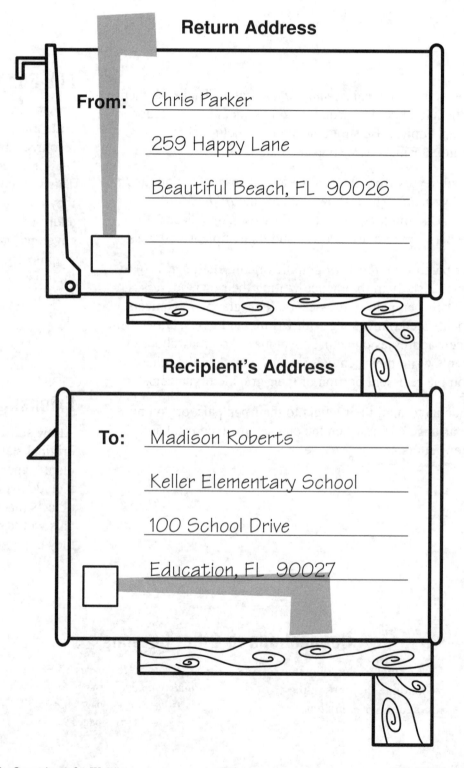

Return Address

From: Chris Parker

259 Happy Lane

Beautiful Beach, FL 90026

Recipient's Address

To: Madison Roberts

Keller Elementary School

100 School Drive

Education, FL 90027

Memory Makers Graphic Organizer

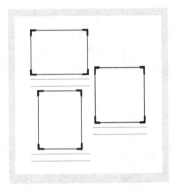

Skills Connection

Type of Writing— narrative

Publishing—drawing pictures and writing captions to show main ideas

Bloom's Level— Application (See page 8 for a description.)

Working with Young Students: Rather than asking younger students to draw three pictures to show the main ideas found in their *narratives*, require them to only draw one. This way, they can do one main idea for the entire *narrative*.

Why Use the Graphic Organizer

- Understanding main idea is often a difficult skill for students. The *Memory Makers* graphic organizer allows students to first draw pictures of the main ideas found in their narratives, and then write captions to those pictures, thus writing the main ideas from their *narratives*.

How to Use the Graphic Organizer

1. Distribute copies of a sample *narrative*. Explain to students what a main idea is. Read the narrative aloud. Ask the class to state the main idea of the narrative.

2. Tell students that finding the main idea in writings and readings is often difficult. Therefore, they are going to use graphic organizers to help them determine the main ideas of their own *narratives*. Place the *Memory Makers Overhead* so that students can see it. Then, draw pictures on the overhead from the sample *narrative* that would show the main ideas found in the *narrative*. Ask students to create captions for the pictures. Write the captions, or main ideas, under the "photos" on the overhead.

3. Distribute the *Memory Makers* graphic organizers (page 120) to the students. Have students compose a short *narrative*. Then, have them draw three pictures to show the main ideas of their *narratives*, and then write captions for those pictures. After students have completed their graphic organizers, allow them to cut out the "photos" and captions and glue them on the bottom of their *narrative* final copies.

ELL Support

Give ELL students more examples of finding main ideas using other *narratives*. This will help them summarize the main ideas for their own *narratives*.

Extension Idea

Encourage students to create entire "photo albums" with more than just the three pictures from their graphic organizers. Have them write captions for all of the pictures in their photo albums.

Name _____

Memory Makers

Directions: Draw three pictures to show the main ideas of your narrative. Then, write captions, or the main ideas, below the pictures.

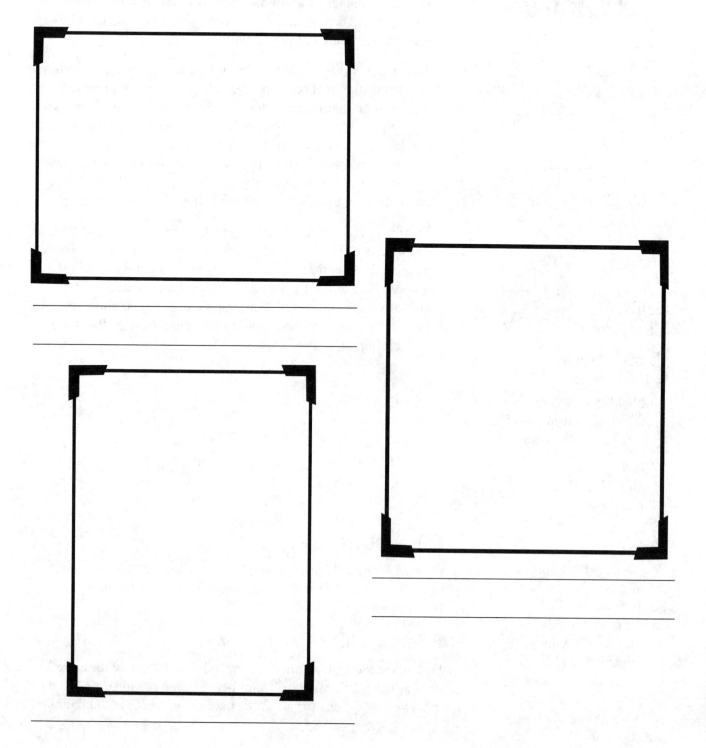

Family Memory Makers

Standard/Objective

- **Publishing:** Knows the main ideas or themes of a story. (McREL Language Arts, Standard 6.4)
- Students will create "photographs" and captions using their *Memory Makers* graphic organizers to show the main ideas of their family *narratives*.

The Lesson

1. Read the following paragraph aloud to the class: "For Halloween this year, I dressed up like a pirate. I put on a pirate patch and a pirate hat. Then, I went trick-or-treating with my brother and sister. We told jokes to get our candy. My treasure chest soon became full. So, we went home. Mom let me eat some of my candy. I ate too much! I got a stomachache."

2. Discuss the concept of main idea with the students. Then, ask them what the main ideas are in the paragraph you read. What pictures could you draw to show the main ideas? Use the *Memory Makers Overhead* to allow students to draw pictures of the main ideas found in the paragraph. Then, ask the class to create captions for those main ideas. Write the captions on the overhead as well. Next, compare the main ideas the students developed with those on the sample graphic organizer (page 122).

3. Distribute students' family moments drafts. Ask them to create final copies of their *narratives*. Then, give each student a copy of the *Memory Makers* graphic organizer (page 120). Have them complete their organizers, creating "photos" and captions of the main ideas found in their *narratives*. Then, allow them to cut out the photos and captions and place them on their *narrative* final copies.

ELL Support

Give ELL students more examples of finding main ideas using other family memory *narratives*. This will help them summarize the main ideas from their *narratives*.

Extension Idea

Encourage students to create entire "photo albums" of family memories that include more than just the three pictures from their graphic organizers. Have them write captions for all of the pictures in their photo albums.

Connections to Other Lessons

Please refer to the following lessons to continue the steps in the process for creating *narrative* writing pieces.

- *Stories to Tell*—pages 29–30
- *Along the Way*—pages 49–50
- *Mr. Fix It*—pages 73–74
- *Like a Sore Thumb*—pages 89–90

Name _____

Memory Makers for Family Moments

Directions: Draw three pictures to show the main ideas of your narrative. Then, write captions, or the main ideas, below the pictures.

I dressed up as a pirate for Halloween.

_____

I ate too much of my Halloween candy

and became sick!

_____

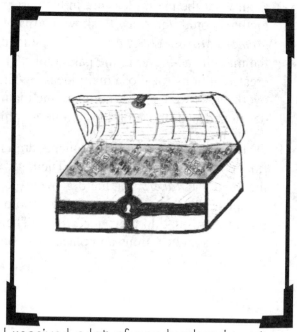

I received a lot of candy when I went

trick-or-treating.

_____

Art courtesy of Jaime Ortiz

Tell Me a Story Graphic Organizer

Skills Connection

Type of Writing— picture books

Publishing— identifying problems, setting, and characters in other's writings

Bloom's Level— Analysis (See page 8 for a description.)

Working with Young Students: Rather than asking younger students to focus on all three elements: problem, setting, and characters, choose just one element for students to discuss on their graphic organizers.

Why Use the Graphic Organizer

- The *Tell Me a Story* graphic organizer gives students the opportunity to analyze peers' writings, as well as ensuring their own comprehension of a story as they list the problems, characters, and setting.

How to Use the Graphic Organizer

1. Distribute students' drafts of stories they have written. Then, explain to the students that they will be turning their rough drafts into final copies in the form of *picture books*, with illustrations to go on each page of their books. Allow students time to create their final copies in class.

2. Display the *Tell Me a Story Overhead*. Explain to students the concepts of setting, character, and plot. Then, read a short *picture book* to the class. Have the students identify the three elements and record them on the overhead.

3. Distribute the *Tell Me a Story* graphic organizers (page 124). Allow students to trade books with partners. Then, have their partners analyze their peers' *picture books* by completing the *Tell Me a Story* graphic organizers. Allow students to discuss their organizers with their partners.

ELL Support

Place ELL students with higher-level classmates that can help them as they analyze the *picture books*.

Extension Idea

Challenge students to create pictures that are abstract, or that copy the techniques of artists such as Eric Carle. This will add more interesting pictures to their books. They may also choose to use photos in their *picture books*.

Name _____

Tell Me a Story

Directions: Read your partner's picture book. Then, identify the setting, problem, and characters using the spaces below.

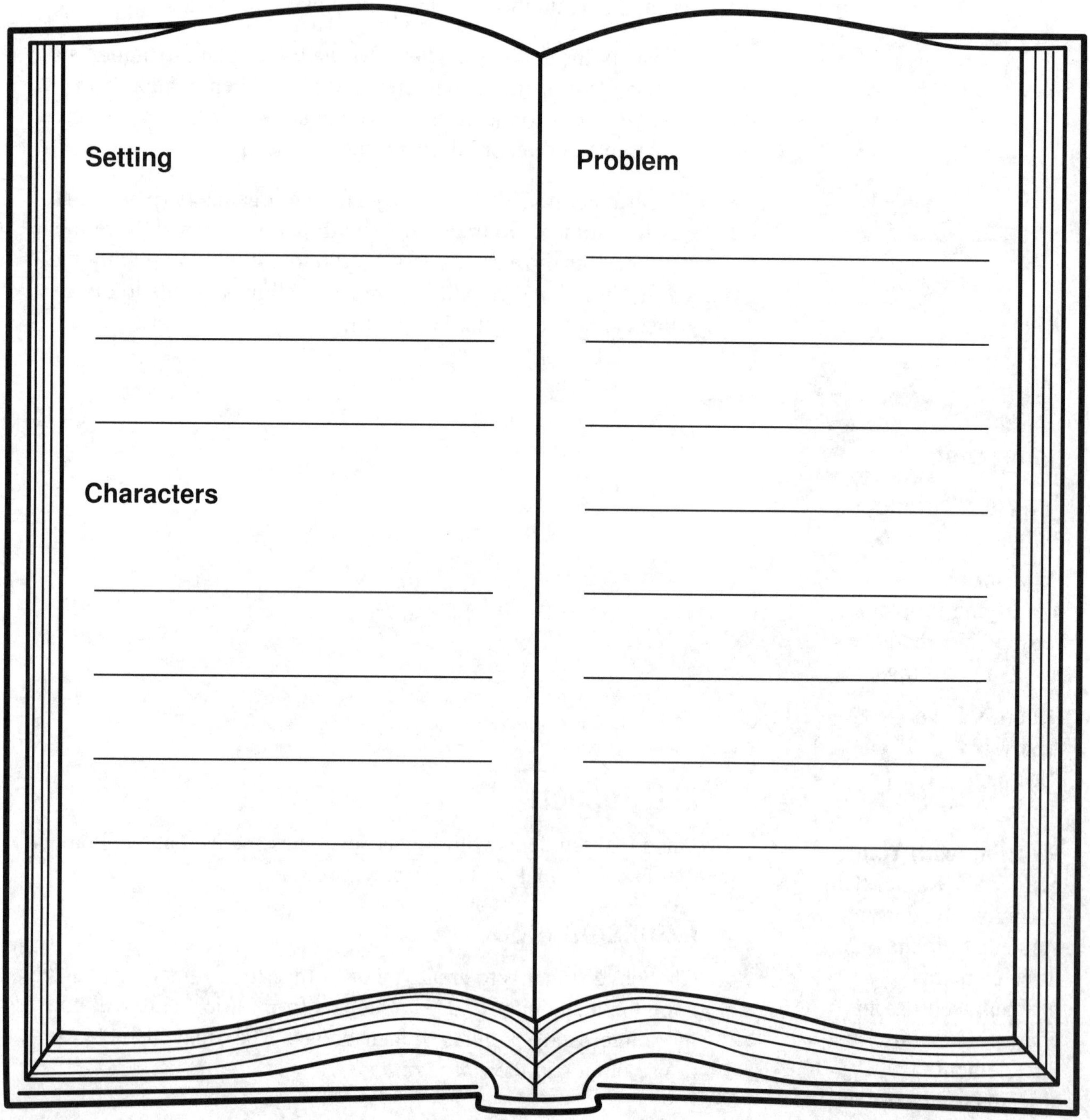

Setting

_____

_____

_____

Characters

_____

_____

_____

_____

Problem

_____

_____

_____

_____

_____

_____

Tell Me a Family Story

Standard/Objective

- **Publishing:** Knows setting, main characters, main events, sequence, and problems in stories. (McREL Language Arts, Standard 6.3)
- Students will analyze their peers' *picture books* as they identify the setting, character, and problem using the *Tell Me a Story* graphic organizers.

The Lesson

1. Read *Olivia* by Ian Falconer to the class. Then, place the *Tell Me a Story Overhead* so that students can see it. Explain to the class the concepts of setting, problem, and characters of a story. Then, ask them if the story you read had all three elements. Identify them using the overhead. You may also use the sample graphic organizer (page 126) to show students the setting, problem, and characters in the story.

2. Give students their family *picture book* drafts. Then, have them trade papers with partners. Also distribute the *Tell Me a Story* graphic organizers (page 124). Tell students that they need to read their partners' *picture books*, and analyze them to make sure that they included a problem, setting, and characters. Once students have completed their graphic organizers, allow them to discuss their answers with their partners, stating if all elements were included in the *picture books*.

3. Tell the students that they are now going to create the final copies of their own family *picture books*. They should use their partners' advice in their final copies. Then, have students create their family *picture books*, complete with colorful illustrations.

ELL Support

Place ELL students with higher-level classmates that can help them as they analyze the family *picture books*.

Extension Idea

Challenge students to create pictures that are abstract, or that copy the techniques of artists such as Eric Carle. This will add more interesting pictures to their family *picture books*. They may also choose to use photos in their *picture books* of their family members.

Connections to Other Lessons

Please refer to the following lessons to continue the steps in the process for creating *picture books*.

- *Doorway to Drawings*—pages 33–34
- *Take Action*—pages 53–54
- *Puzzle Pieces*—pages 81–82
- *The Strongest Word*—pages 93–94

Name _____

Tell Me a Story for *Olivia's Family*

Directions: Read your partner's picture book. Then, identify the setting, problems, and characters using the space below.

Setting

Olivia's home, the art

museum, the beach

Characters

Olivia, her mother, her father,

her brother Ian, her cat

Edwin, and her dog Perry

Problem

Olivia must find ways to

entertain herself and her

family.

Having a Ball Graphic Organizer

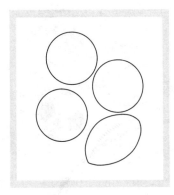

Skills Connection

Type of Writing— poetry

Publishing— incorporating illustrations

Bloom's Level— Synthesis (See page 8 for a description.)

Working with Young Students: Allow younger students to find pictures in magazines that they could trace or cut and paste for their *poetry* pictures.

Why Use the Graphic Organizer

- Illustrations help students visualize their reading and writings. The *Having a Ball* graphic organizer allows students to sketch various illustrations that could be used to represent their poems.

How to Use the Graphic Organizer

1. Read a poem to the class. Then, place the *Having a Ball Overhead* so that students can view it. Ask them what pictures they got in their minds when they heard the poem read to them. Sketch the pictures they describe on the overhead.

2. Distribute the *Having a Ball* graphic organizers (page 128). Have students compose short poems or work with poems they have previously written. Tell students that they need to sketch four pictures on their graphic organizers that would show what is happening in their poems. Once students have created illustrations for their poems, have them circle one illustration on their graphic organizers that they wish to use in their final copies of their poems.

3. Ask students to create final copies of their poems on blank sheets of paper, making all revisions and including their illustrations from their graphic organizers. Then, allow them to share their poems with the class.

ELL Support

Allow ELL students to work with partners when writing their final copies. They can brainstorm ideas for their illustrations with their partners.

Extension Idea

Challenge students to create collages for their poems, using all of the pictures on their graphic organizers.

Name _____

Having a Ball

Directions: Sketch pictures on the balls below that would show what is happening in your poem.

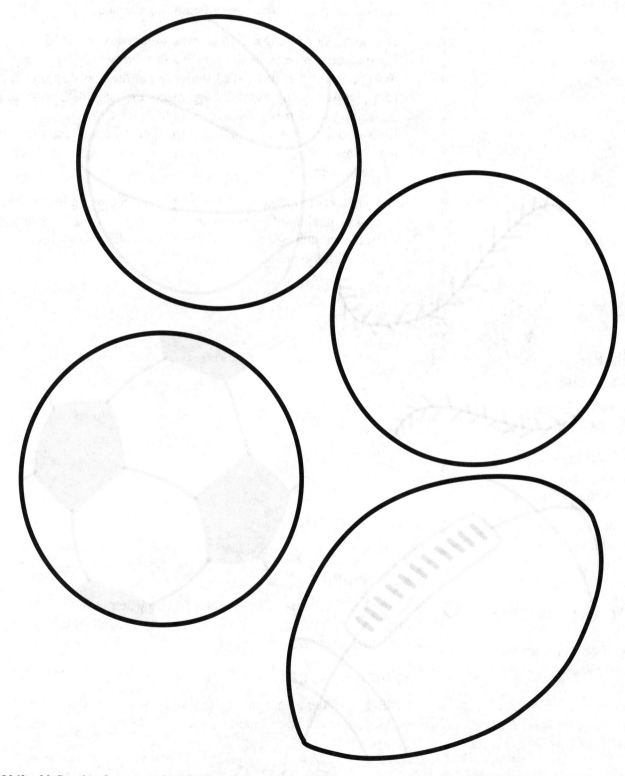

128

Having an Animal Ball

Standard/Objective

- **Publishing:** Uses strategies to edit and publish written work (e.g., incorporates illustrations or photos). (McREL Language Arts, Standard 1.3)
- Students will use their *Having a Ball* graphic organizers to create various illustrations that can be used to show what is happening in their animal poems.

The Lesson

1. Read the following poem to students: "There once was a bee named Lee, who paid a small fee to live in a tree. Though the tree wasn't free, he was as happy as a bee could be." Then, show students the sample graphic organizer (page 130). Ask students if the pictures in the sample show what is happening in the poem. Do the pictures help the students visualize the poem in their minds? Which picture is best for showing what is happening in the poem? Explain to students that illustrations help us get pictures in our minds of what is happening in the things we read.

2. Give each student a copy of the *Having a Ball* graphic organizer (page 128). Then, distribute the students' animal poetry drafts. Have students read their poems, and then sketch pictures that would show what is happening in their poems. Then, have students choose one of their pictures from their graphic organizers to use on their final copies.

3. Give students blank pieces of paper. Allow them to write their final copies of their animal poems, making all revisions. Then, have students draw the pictures they chose from their graphic organizers on their final copies as well. If students wish, allow them to share their animal poems and illustrations with the class.

ELL Support

Allow ELL students to work with partners when writing their animal *poetry* final copies. They can brainstorm ideas for their illustrations with their partners.

Extension Idea

Challenge students to create animal collages for their poems, using all of the pictures on their graphic organizers. They may also find pictures of animals in magazines to include in their collages as well.

Connections to Other Lessons

Please refer to the following lessons to continue the steps in the process for creating *poetry*.

- *The Rhyme Climb*—pages 21–22
- *Poetry in Motion*—pages 57–58
- *At the Car Wash*—pages 85–86
- *Ask Me Anything*—pages 105–106

Name _____

Having a Ball for Animal Poems

Directions: Sketch pictures on the balls below that would show what is happening in your poem.

Art courtesy of Jaime Ortiz

Picture This Graphic Organizer

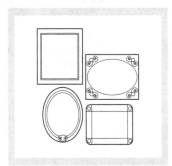

Skills Connection

Type of Writing— informational writing

Publishing—uses mental images to aid in comprehension of writing

Bloom's Level— Evaluation (See page 8 for a description.)

Working with Young Students: Before having younger students read their peers' writings, read a vivid paragraph to the entire class, which is full of descriptions. Then, allow younger students to draw pictures of the mental images they had as they heard the paragraph being read to them.

Why Use the Graphic Organizer

- Visualization and using mental images is extremely important to the comprehension of a text. The graphic organizer, *Picture This,* gives students the opportunity to draw the images they get in their minds as they read their peers' writings. They can then use these images to evaluate the effectiveness of their peers' *informational* writing pieces.

How to Use the Graphic Organizer

1. Read a vivid paragraph from a textbook to the class. As you read, ask the class to close their eyes, to see what images they get in their mind as you read. Display the *Picture This Overhead.* Allow volunteers to draw some of the images they had as you read the paragraph on the overhead. Have the class then evaluate the paragraph, based on how much information was given. Was there enough information to allow images to form in their minds? Did the images help them understand what the text was about? Evaluate the paragraph as a class on the bottom of the graphic organizer.

2. Distribute the *Picture This* graphic organizers (page 132). Have students write an *informational* paragraph, or have them work with a previously written draft.

3. Then, tell the students that they are now going to read their paragraphs to classmates. Each partner should read his or her paragraph aloud. The other partner should draw the images he/she gets onto the graphic organizer. Then, have the students evaluate their partners' paragraphs based on how much information was given.

ELL Support

If ELL students are uncomfortable reading their *informational* writings aloud with their partners, then place them in groups of three. This way, one partner can read the ELL student's writing, while the other partner draws the images he/she gets from the writing.

Extension Idea

As a self evaluation, you may ask students to draw the images they get from their own writings. Have students then evaluate themselves using their *Picture This* graphic organizers.

Name _____

Picture This

Directions: Draw images that you get in your mind as you hear the paragraph read to you. Then, evaluate how informational the paragraph was by circling your answer to the question at the bottom of the page.

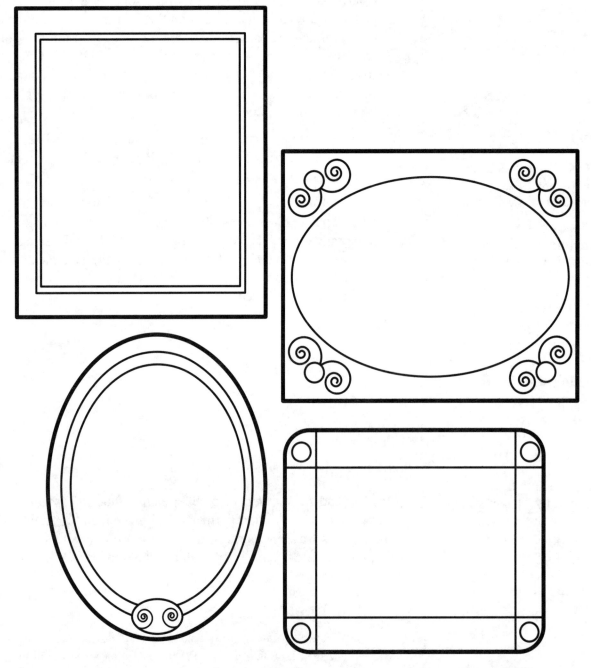

Was there enough information for me to get pictures in my mind?   **YES**   **NO**

Picture My Science Topic

Standard/Objective

- **Publishing:** Uses mental images based on pictures and print to aid in comprehension of text. (McREL Language Arts, Standard 5.1)

- Students will use their *Picture This* graphic organizers to draw the mental images they get when hearing their peers' writings. They will then evaluate their peers' *informational* writings by stating if enough information was given to form mental images.

The Lesson

1. Read the following paragraph to the students: "The four seasons are spring, summer, fall, and winter. In the spring, it is warm. The trees begin to get their leaves. Then, summer comes. The weather is hot, and the trees have all of their leaves. Next, we have fall. Fall is called autumn, too. The trees lose their leaves. It begins to get cooler. Then, winter arrives. It is cold, and there are no leaves on the trees." As you read, have students close their eyes to picture the things mentioned in the paragraph.

2. Then, display the *Picture This Overhead.* Have several volunteers draw the images they got in their minds as the paragraph was read to them. Have the class vote in order to evaluate the paragraph on the bottom of the organizer. Next, show students the sample graphic organizer (page 134) to see if their images were similar to those found on the sample. What pictures besides trees could have been drawn?

3. Distribute students' science rough drafts. Ask them to create final copies of their *informational* writings. Also give each student a copy of the *Picture This* graphic organizer (page 132). Have students read their writings to partners, so that their partners can form images and evaluate the writings. After students have completed their images and evaluations on their graphic organizers, have them share their images and evaluations with their partners.

ELL Support

If ELL students are uncomfortable reading their science *informational* writings aloud with their partners, then place them in groups of three. This way, one partner can read the ELL student's writing, while the other partner draws the images he/she gets from the writing.

Extension Idea

As a self evaluation, you may ask students to draw the scientific images they get from their own writings. Have students then evaluate themselves using their *Picture This* graphic organizers.

Connections to Other Lessons

Please refer to the following lessons to continue the steps in the process for creating *informational* writing pieces.

- *Shopping for Ideas*—pages 17–18
- *Words from the Wise*—pages 45–46
- *At the End of the Rope*—pages 77–78
- *One More Time*—pages 101–102

Name _____

Picture This for the Four Seasons Science Topic

Directions: Draw images that you get in your mind as you hear the paragraph read to you. Then, evaluate how informational the paragraph was by circling your answer to the question at the bottom of the page.

Art courtesy of Jaime Ortiz

Was there enough information for me to get pictures in my mind? (**YES**) **NO**

Works Cited

Bos, C. N., and P. L. Anders. (1992). Using interactive teaching and learning strategies to promote text comprehension and content learning for students with learning disabilities. *International Journal of Disability, Development and Education* 39:225–238.

Boyle, J. R., and M. Weishaar. (1997). The effects of expert-generated versus student-generated cognitive organizers on the reading comprehension of students with learning disabilities. *Learning Disabilities Research & Practice* 12:228–235.

Brookbank, D., S. Grover, K. Kullberg, and C. Strawser. (1999). Improving student achievement through organization of student learning. Chicago: Master's Action Research Project, Saint Xavier University and IRI/Skylight.

DeWispelaere, C. and J. Kossack. (1996). Improving student higher order thinking skills through the use of graphic organizers. Elk Grove Village, IL: Master's Thesis, Saint Xavier University.

Doyle, C. S. (1999). The use of graphic organizers to improve comprehension of learning disabled students in social studies. Union, NJ: Master of Arts Research Project, Kean University.

Gallego, M. A., G. Z. Duran, and D. J. Scanlon. (1990). Interactive teaching and learning: Facilitating learning disabled students' progress from novice to expert. In *Literacy theory and research: Analyses from multiple paradigms: Thirty-ninth yearbook of the National Reading Conference*, J. Zutell and S. McCormick, eds., (pp. 311–319). Chicago: National Reading Conference.

Gallick-Jackson, S. A. (1997). Improving narrative writing skills, composition skills, and related attitudes among second grade students by integrating word processing, graphic organizers, and art into a process approach to writing. Fort Lauderdale, FL: Master of Science Practicum Project, Nova Southeastern University.

Gardill, M. C. and A. K. Jitendra. (1999). Advanced story map instruction: Effects on the reading comprehension of students with learning disabilities. *The Journal of Special Education* 33:2–17.

Griffin, C., L. Malone, and E. Kameenui. (1995). Effects of graphic organizer instruction on fifth-grade students. *Journal of Educational Research* 89:98–107.

Griffin, C., D. C. Simmons, and E. J. Kameenui. (1991). Investigating the effectiveness of graphic organizer instruction on the comprehension and recall of science content by students with learning disabilities. *Journal of Reading, Writing, and Learning Disabilities International* 7:355–376.

Jensen, E. (1998). *Teaching with the Brain in Mind*. Alexandria, VA: Association for Supervision and Curriculum Development.

Moore, D. and J. Readence. (1984). A quantitative and qualitative review of graphic organizer research. *Journal of Educational Research* 78:11–17.

National Reading Panel. (2000). *Teaching children to read: An evidence-based assessment of the scientific research literature on reading and its implications for reading instruction.*

Olsen, K. D. (1995). *Science Continuum of Concepts for Grades K–6.* Books for Educators: Covington, WA: from http://www.nichd.nih.gov/publications/nrp/smallbook.htm, (accessed April 4, 2005).

Ritchie, D. and C. Volkl. (2000). Effectiveness of two generative learning strategies in the science classroom. *School Science and Mathematics* 100:83–89.

Sinatra, R. C., J. Stahl-Glemake, and D. N. Berg. (1984). Improving reading comprehension of disabled readers through semantic mapping. *Reading Teacher* 38:22–29.

Sprenger, M. (1999). *Learning and memory: The brain in action.* Alexandria, VA: Association for Supervision and Development.

Graphic Organizer Flip Book

What Is a Flip Book?

The Graphic Organizer Flip Book on the following pages is a compact, informative chart that shows differentiated organizers at a glance. It is a handy tool for busy teachers who want to create lessons using graphic organizers. It also divides the graphic organizers into the levels of Bloom's Taxonomy, which enables the teacher to challenge students to think on all levels within the cognitive domain.

This flip book is like a reference guide for teachers. The tabbed pages make it easy to flip to the desired level of Bloom's Taxonomy. On each page in the flip book are key verbs as well as thumbnail images of graphic organizers associated with that level of Bloom's Taxonomy. On the last page of the flip book is a list of leading questions that correlate with all the levels of Bloom's Taxonomy.

Directions for Making the Flip Book

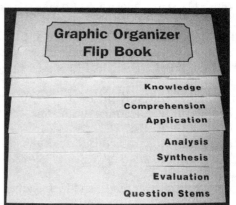

1. Carefully rip the next four sheets of paper (pages 137–144) out of the book along the perforated cut near the spine.

2. Fold each page along the dotted gray line. You need to fold the odd pages over the even sides of each page. For your reference, the page numbers are included above the gray fold lines.

3. After all the pages have been folded carefully, place them in order. The sheet with pages 137–138 is on the top or outside. The inside or middle sheet is pages 143–144.

4. At this point, your flip book should have the six levels of Bloom's Taxonomy listed down the right side. The last flap should read Question Stems. If you don't see these words down the right side, you probably folded one of the pieces of paper the wrong way. Take the book apart and check each fold.

5. You may want to staple the book together to make it easier to use. If you do staple it, make sure you staple very close to the fold so that you can read all the text.

6. Keep in mind, as you look at your finished flip book, that imperfections in the printing of the pages might affect the way the pages line up. You can refold individual pages before stapling it to make the book line up better.

Graphic Organizer
Flip Book

Evaluation

Question stems for evaluation activities include:

- Do you agree or disagree with . . . ?
- Judge how well this . . . ?
- How effective was . . . ?
- What would you recommend for . . . ?

- Why did that person . . . ?
- Can you justify . . . ?
- In what ways can you support . . . ?
- Which would you select and why?

Synthesis

Question stems for synthesis activities include:

- Can you write a poem/song about . . . ?
- What would happen if . . . ?
- In what ways could you improve . . . ?
- How many ways can you . . . ?

- Can you invent a way to . . . ?
- How would you test . . . ?
- What new uses are there for . . . ?
- How would you change . . . ?

Analysis

Question stems for analysis activities include:

- In what ways is ____ related to . . . ?
- How was this similar to . . . ?
- What is the theme of . . . ?
- How would you classify . . . ?

- What was the problem with . . . ?
- How does ____ work?
- What are the parts of . . . ?
- Why do you think . . . ?

Knowledge Skills

This cognitive skill requires that students:

- recall or locate information
- remember something previously learned
- memorize information

When asking questions that require knowledge, the following verbs are used:

arrange	define	describe	duplicate	identify	label	list
locate	match	memorize	name	order	recall	recite
recognize	relate	remember	repeat	reproduce	state	tell

Knowledge

Question stems for knowledge activities include:

- What is . . . ?
- When did _____ happen?
- How many . . . ?
- Can you remember . . . ?
- Who was . . . ?
- Where did _____ happen?
- What is the meaning of . . . ?
- How would you describe . . . ?

Comprehension

Question stems for comprehension activities include:

- How would you summarize . . . ?
- What was the main idea of . . . ?
- Can you compare and contrast . . . ?
- What facts support . . . ?
- Can you define . . . ?
- How could you describe . . . ?
- Who was a key character in . . . ?
- Can you restate in your own words . . . ?

Application

Question stems for application activities include:

- How would you classify . . . ?
- What questions might you ask . . . ?
- How would you use a . . . ?
- Could you substitute something for . . . ?
- Could the same event have happened in . . . ?
- In what ways could you apply . . . ?
- What would happen if . . . ?
- What would you change if . . . ?

outside fold
page 139

Graphic Organizers for Knowledge

Shopping for Ideas
pages 15–18

A Shower of Words
pages 39–42

The Name Game
pages 63–66

Like a Sore Thumb
pages 87–90

Share the Love
pages 111–114

Knowledge

Graphic Organizers for Evaluation

Snapshots of Me
pages 35–38

Lending a Hand
pages 107–110

Building a Letter
pages 59–62

Picture This
pages 131–134

At the Car Wash
pages 83–86

---

inside fold
page 140

Comprehension Skills

This cognitive skill requires that students:

- understand and explain facts
- demonstrate basic understanding of concepts and curriculum
- translate to other words
- grasp the meaning
- interpret information
- explain what happened in their own words or pictures

When asking questions that require comprehension, the following verbs are used:

report	restate	review	select	summarize	translate
express	generalize	identify	indicate	locate	predict	recognize
classify	describe	discuss	distinguish	edit	estimate	explain

Evaluation Skills

This cognitive skill requires that students:

- make judgments based on evidence
- judge the value of something using criteria
- support their judgments
- judge the value of material for a given purpose
- examine a person/policy/event and tell whether it measures up to a certain standard

When asking questions that require evaluation, the following verbs are used:

appraise	argue	assess	compare	conclude
criticize	critique	defend	estimate	evaluate
give opinions	interpret	judge	justify	predict
prioritize	rate	recommend	support	value

Graphic Organizers for Comprehension

The Rhyme Climb
pages 19–22

Words from the Wise
pages 43–46

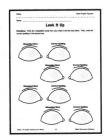

Look it Up
pages 67–70

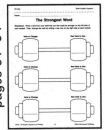

The Strongest Word
pages 91–94

In the Mail
pages 115–118

Comprehension

Application Skills

This cognitive skill requires that students:

- use prior learning to solve a problem or to answer a question
- transfer knowledge learned in one situation to another
- use material in new and concrete situations
- apply the lessons of the past to situations today

When asking questions that require application, the following verbs are used:

apply	build	choose	compute	cook	demonstrate
discover	dramatize	employ	illustrate	operate	practice
prepare	produce	schedule	sketch	solve	write
use					

inside fold
page 142

Graphic Organizers for Synthesis

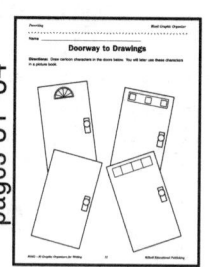

Doorway to Drawings pages 31–34

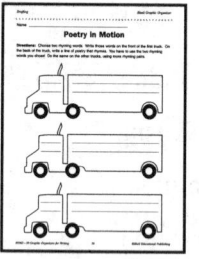

Poetry in Motion pages 55–58

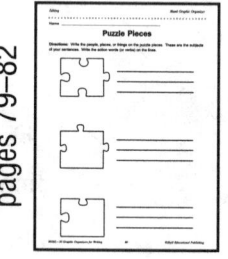

Puzzle Pieces pages 79–82

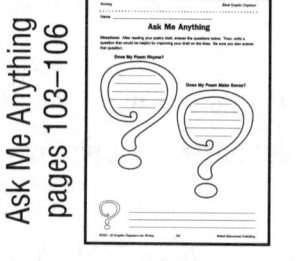

Ask Me Anything pages 103–106

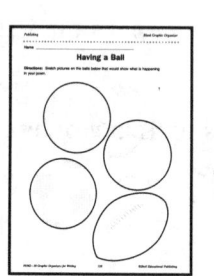

Having a Ball pages 127–130

Synthesis

Synthesis Skills

This cognitive skill requires that students:

- understand and explain facts
- create new ideas by pulling parts of the information together
- reform individual parts to make a new whole
- take a jumble of facts and add them up to make sense

When asking questions that require synthesis, the following verbs are used:

arrange	assemble	categorize	collect	combine
compile	compose	construct	create	design
develop	forecast	formulate	hypothesize	imagine
invent	manage	organize	plan	prepare
propose	rearrange	reconstruct	set up	write

Graphic Organizers for Application

Bright Ideas
pages 23–26

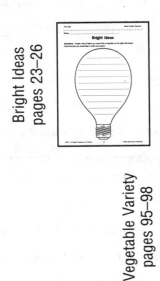

Along the Way
pages 47–50

Mr. Fix It
pages 71–74

Vegetable Variety
pages 95–98

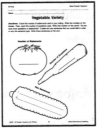

Memory Makers
pages 119–122

Application

Analysis Skills

This cognitive skill requires that students:

- see in-depth relationships between and among parts of the information
- understand how parts relate to a whole
- understand structure and motive
- note fallacies
- break down material into its component parts so that its organizational structure may be understood
- take a complicated situation and break it down into its parts

When asking questions that require analysis, the following verbs are used:

categorize	classify	compare	contrast	diagram
differentiate	distinguish	examine	illustrate	investigate
outline	separate	solve		

---

inside fold
page 144

Graphic Organizers for Analysis

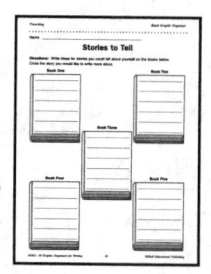

Stories to Tell
pages 27–30

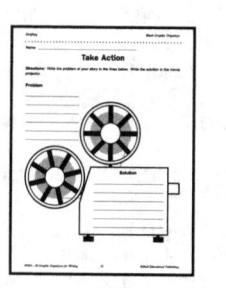

Take Action
pages 51–54

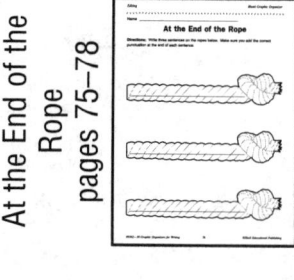

At the End of the Rope
pages 75–78

One More Time
pages 99–102

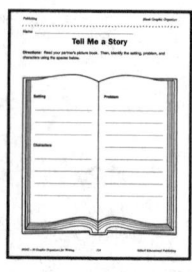

Tell Me a Story
pages 123–126

Analysis